THE QUANTUM
LIFE

THERE IS A BETTER WAY TO LIVE

Dr. M. Teri Daunter

BALBOA.PRESS

A DIVISION OF HAY HOUSE

Balboa Press books may be ordered through booksellers or by contacting:

Balboa Press
A Division of Hay House
1663 Liberty Drive
Bloomington, IN 47403
www.balboapress.com
844-682-1282

Because of the dynamic nature of the Internet, any web addresses or links contained in this book may have changed since publication and may no longer be valid. The views expressed in this work are solely those of the author and do not necessarily reflect the views of the publisher, and the publisher hereby disclaims any responsibility for them.

The author of this book does not dispense medical advice or prescribe the use of any technique as a form of treatment for physical, emotional, or medical problems without the advice of a physician, either directly or indirectly. The intent of the author is only to offer information of a general nature to help you in your quest for emotional and spiritual well-being. In the event you use any of the information in this book for yourself, which is your constitutional right, the author and the publisher assume no responsibility for your actions.

Scripture quotations marked KJV are from the Holy Bible, King James Version (Authorized Version). First published in 1611. Quoted from the KJV Classic Reference Bible, Copyright © 1983 by The Zondervan Corporation.

Any people depicted in stock imagery provided by Getty Images are models, and such images are being used for illustrative purposes only. Certain stock imagery © Getty Images.

Print information available on the last page.

ISBN: 978-1-9822-6797-1 (sc)
ISBN: 978-1-9822-6799-5 (hc)
ISBN: 978-1-9822-6798-8 (e)

Library of Congress Control Number: 2021908284

Balboa Press rev. date: 05/24/2021

CONTENTS

DEDICATION

This book is dedicated to SOURCE who
is the giver of all grace and invokes and anchors into the earth
Infinite Creative Intelligence

and to

BABAJI
My Spiritual Teacher
with a most delightful sense of humor
who has already achieved
pure potentiality and through whose inspiration and
inner consciousness has opened the door for me to
realize my True Being

I AM
that
I AM

INTRODUCTION

The Quantum Life presents you with an energy/medical/spiritual model that invites you to awaken progressively toward a greater reality and toward your True Being because you live in a world that is psycho–spiritually crippled! The Quantum Life, a path of self-discovery and self-realization, invites you to walk the Divine life so that we can walk each other Home in freedom, spontaneity, and knowledge of our immortality. In the manner of a kaleidoscope, which often reminds me of a metaphysical symbol of Consciousness, you will have multiple reflections. You will release blocked creativity, endow your life with meaning and give yourself the opportunity to see yourself in the bigger scope of life by connecting to your True Self.

If we are to awaken together, however, The Quantum Life is needed to end your deceptions and innocence and help you to face life without illusions. Do not let them get to you at the soulic level any longer. Let us together be witness and part of the dissolution of orthodoxy and move from the dark forces to the Light. Be a part of the inward revolution. There is a more beautiful world than your heart knows is possible.

The Quantum Life with its inherent psychology of Consciousness prods you to think about who you are and why you are here. Life is about movement, it instructs, and the quantum life is about its ancillary relationship to the initiator of this movement. If you want to progress by knowing the truth, continue to read The Quantum Life as it shall dispel your original falsehoods and all contingent falsehoods which have covered the original Truth. You will see that the basic Newtonian concepts with which you have lived all your life and accepted, that made your security, have only been a dam obstructing the flow of your spiritual energy because Newtonian concepts do not operate in the greater Infinity. Furthermore, it is impossible for you to just remain where you are. You either regress

1

or you progress by your choices. However, I am of the assumption that the old concepts must give way to new concepts if our world is going to progress rather than regress into some primitive beginning. If you have a sincere motivation to learn and to be an open channel, The Quantum Life will help you knock down the dam to allow you to receive the intelligence of the movement of the river and all the molecules it carries through its waves. Your sincerity will align you with Infinite Intelligence. In this way you will pioneer a new frontier for your soul. You are an integer of the Infinite. Raise your binoculars and see a vaster distance.

The Quantum Life will teach you the physics of your inner life and provide you with a transcendent life changing power. It will show you how you span two dimensions simultaneously. You will learn to operate from a much larger computer with infinite information. The Quantum Life will repeatedly emphasize that the only Source of truth resides within you, nowhere else. The Quantum Life will further show you how your aggressive patriarchal world has made decisions for you of enormous harm which has been the greatest crime against your spirituality. It will pierce through your sense and physical consciousness because as long as you continue to confine yourself to merely the physical, you will only relate to the material world. The Quantum Life is not interested in what you do but what you are. It will repeatedly emphasize that you alone are responsible!

Are you hurting enough to listen and begin to create yourself anew? Then let this emergency be your emergence so that you can find your life of magic by creating a great leap through a mass Consciousness shift from your global wounding. Consciousness is your Infinite Seer. The Quantum Life will show you how you have been betrayed by a system that has brainwashed you; at the same time The Quantum Life will create a climate in which you can flower and will plug you into a system of Oneness. How long it takes you to realize that you are a part of the Greater Whole is inconsequential. In earth times, in which your physical third dimensional self lives, which is not your true nor complete definition, it could be many years. Your physical body is merely your video screen of your computer. In the fourth dimension in which your soul lives, it is momentary. Awakening, awareness and recognition of yourself as an interdimensional being are of importance to be able to live in a physical anatomy with a non-physical mentality. Awakening requires that you understand your role in the universe and how your thoughts and actions set all the laws of this universe in motion. Through this process is how you become a highly realized individual. You will learn in The Quantum Life of your transcended states of consciousness, the fourth and fifth dimension, the sea of energy, through meditation. Albert Einstein received the mathematical symbology for his formula $E = MC2$ through this fourth dimensional movement of energy. This is your wake-up period!

The Quantum Life deals with the supraphysical, and at times makes for uncomfortable yet stimulating reading because it points out for you the immorality and cognitive dissonance of orthodoxy. It is provocative, intellectually and spiritually challenging. It will trigger you and it will awaken you. It will dispel the false view of what you are as an individual in the universe which has rendered you false and unhappy. If you allow it, it will help you shed your mask and embrace who you are unless you do not want your comfortable little world disrupted! This book is about the liberation of your soul as it awakens you to a profounder self-knowledge. Let us open the dialogue so you can see how you have been chained and hampered and living a life of fiction. You have gotten into this chain gang by forgetting who you are and lost consciousness of your True Self. You can cut your shackles by remembering who you are and know that no one but you is the repository of Truth. Why is this important? Because it has an effect on how you think; and, consequently, on the decisions that you make and how you interpret any data. Therefore, it is critical that you meld your mind with the intelligent consciousness of Infinite Intelligence.

You have been helplessly limited because you have self-identified with the body when you are actually limitless. You are just in your own way enslaved to the concept of convention which has clouded your understanding placing you in a state of spiritual starvation. You have become a part of the collective structure and regressed in a crowd of destructive thinking. You have become a part of the crowd but not a part of the Oneness. The former is fiction, unsatisfying and barren. Stop cultivating and spreading this fiction because it is preventing you from knowing who you are. Do not stay in bondage any longer! Master the Truth and Light your soul. The Truth can only come from your own personal experience. Look within! There is a better way to live.

The fact that you are reading this book tells me that you are actually already in the midst of your awakening, your emergence. The Quantum Life does not expect everyone to follow the same path for reaching spiritual evolution. Therefore, it provides innumerable ways for your progressive evolution. With persistence and dedication you will integrate an infinite number of factors into your consciousness and you will achieve spiritual solvency. There is a tolerance and inclusiveness characteristic in the quantum way of life.

QUANTUM SPIRITUALITY

Quantum spirituality is the physics of the Infinite and provides an exciting vision of spirituality that uses the principles of quantum physics. It is founded on non-locality, quantum entanglement, and discontinuous quantum leaps in Consciousness. It unmasks and depathologizes the disease of orthodoxy and directs you into your inner core (potentia). Quantum spirituality teaches you no dogmas and provides you no shackles. It awakens you to the fact that ninety-eight percent of your life is coming from a collective hypnosis and conditioning. This conditioning keeps pulling you deeper and deeper into the fractal, trapping you in a loop. This awareness will have far reaching implications for you as an individual and on a collective scale. Your body will benefit greatly when you get off the roller coaster and you become more consciously aware. Everything depends on you!

Quantum spirituality, informed by quantum physics, reveals the limitations and flaws of Newtonian physics as applied to conventional growth. The classic Newtonian model creates a very limited view of humanity and does not consider our potential to evolve beyond our physical bodies. When you accept quantum spirituality you no longer allow Newtonian physics to dictate how you view yourself or how you can be treated. Quantum spirituality shows that spiritual evolution is a multi-dimensional experience. No one can dictate your beliefs without your permission!

Quantum spirituality owes its debt to C. G. Jung, a Swiss Psychiatrist and a student of Freud, who conducted significant clinical research on the "collective unconscious" and how this all played out in dynamic patterns as well as organizing principles in our lives, spirituality, physical health and decision-making. Jung discovered that Consciousness (the fifth dimension) and matter (the third dimension) flowed in and out with one another and were in a constant dance with each other. This dance influences both dimensions reciprocally, similar to quantum entanglement, so that it becomes hard to distinguish one from the other. Or as William Butler Yeats, the poet, has often written, "you cannot tell the dancer from the dance." This is exactly the process that occurs through meditation where you enter silence and merge with Consciousness. Through the silence you will learn the connection to the main river so that you can connect to the Ocean.

You are not a biological computer, therefore, and you have transcending abilities far beyond linear causality. Life is not linear. It is granulated. Non-linear experiences profoundly influence your spiritual development. Become more aware of this dimension and cultivate it, because you can no longer develop spiritually through the conventional orthodox model, which we shall unmask, with its inherent limitations. Accepting quantum spirituality is critical, not just for you as an individual, but also for our planet.

The orthodox model is a spiritual conceptual straightjacket predicated on fear and dogmatic positions. It is harvesting your soul. Orthodoxy has been very divisive and needs to move to the spiritual part of life. Proponents of orthodoxy are inflexible and unable to help you with your evolution because they keep you living in a box. These organizations are all models of altruistic presumptuousness without a vision. This is why so many individuals have become disillusioned with them and walked away. Orthodoxy has become unconvincing.

You need to ignore orthodoxy until such time that those who accept it show clarity of thinking and are freed from narrowness. Orthodoxy is unenlightened. Relinquish orthodoxy and its damning selfishness. The inner law is the law of the awakened soul. Its morals are so much greater than any mortal could ever possibly conceive. It is your inner divine language and it will never fail you. It comes through your Silence. It has no voice. It is like divine music with deep meaning for every note. These will be drops from the Ocean brought to you directly to your heart. Drop by drop you will have the entire Ocean in your heart. Then you will totally merge with the Ocean, and by reaching the depth of the Ocean, you will achieve the goal of every spiritual being: Self-realization.

Orthodoxy is self-serving, self-satisfying and self-glorifying. If you are too inflexible to make a shift, then stay stuck in your current crisis and your self-made prison. But if you wish to find your power to leave it, start by studying this prison in which you are encapsulated. Use quantum spirituality as your guiding map to your spiritual evolution; it evolves constantly, is flexible and aligns with the findings on Consciousness research and the multi-dimensional individual. It teaches you that we differ only in appearance. The Quantum Life will secure you in the truth of Eckhart that "the eye with which I see God is the same eye with which God sees me."

Quantum spirituality gives you an expanded vision of all that you can be that goes far beyond the limits of your physical body because it cuts through concepts and dogmas. It takes you into a state of pure potentiality. It will help you rediscover ancient knowledge of transpersonal fields for your spiritual growth held by Shamanism and Taoism who have helped us discover the beyond that is within. Buddhism and Christianity, Islam and Judaism who have helped us discover the God that is within. These perennial philosophies in quantum spirituality are proving invaluable in our spiritual evolution as well as our physical and mental health. In quantum spirituality every moment becomes a moment of crystal worship rather than at a certain time and certain day within four walls. Break through the walls of your eggshell. Emerge into the quantum world by unlearning all that you have learned.

Do not suppress any longer that which you know is true. Do not hold on any longer to that which is not serving you well. End the betrayal. End the manipulation. Get into your full vision and see with total clarity all that you are and all that you can become. Move away from norms and ideologies. I guarantee you that when you find out that everything you have been told is not correct and the people you trusted are not the people you thought they were, you will be lost. You will have to find out for yourself the truth. It is not easy. You will witness the hand of God because you are a fifth

7

dimensional Light Being. Are you fearful of getting into a personal, spiritual, and emotional crisis? Well, that is the most favorable time to bring about change. When things are going smoothly, we tend to become stagnant and comfortable and not make changes in our lives. In the midst of a crisis when things begin to break down is when true change becomes possible. Take full advantage of it rather than being afraid of it. There is a better way to live. Give credibility to what comes from within you.

Had I not given credibility some years ago to a sudden vision of a dirty soiled aura (an energy field represented by color), which appeared around a female person's crown and upper body during therapy, a female who outwardly sounded very believable, the wrong person would have been imprisoned by the judicial system. Our physical body is surrounded by an energy field that provides us information. This information is available to everyone. The subtle information in this woman's aura was negative, even though on the surface she appeared as very nice and sincere. This energetic language continued to speak to me. The consistent appearance of the muddy aura circling her crown chakra (sahasrara) and her third eye chakra (ajna) forewarned me from the beginning of the consultation of the disparity between her spoken word and her energy field.

Our chakras are our energy fields and the metaphysical expressions of the energy in our physical bodies. We need to keep our chakras healthy if we are going to stay physically healthy. They are our power centers and electrical rods that ground us into our physical body. Chakras, ladders of Consciousness, are the architecture of our human body as well as related to our spiritual development.

The ability to see this patient's aura, and trusting in all that I AM, allowed me to diagnose her general condition of disparity, incongruence and dishonesty. Seeing the aura, a subtle energy phenomenon, defied ordinary explanation but which my intuition recognized. Listening and trusting my intuition unfolded a new dimension alerting me to continue to probe more deeply and investigate further as the expert witness in this very sensitive clinical court case. I did not let my mind override my intuition or subtle sensing. By giving credibility to the vision of this patient's energy field, a functional creative inspiration which proved accurate, I was able to diagnose her general condition beyond her verbal reporting and reached a just and fair conclusion for all concerned.

These visions are not gifted to me only. You are capable of the very same experiences because we are all unlimited in our visions. Nicola Tesla's contributions and designs of his first generator appeared to him in visions. Dr. Spudick, professor of biochemistry at Stanford University, was studying mutation-induced hypercontractility when the image of a mesa came to him in a vision in his sleep which sparked insight into this deadly heart disorder. The dream advanced the progress of his research by many years. Giacomo Puccini, creator of the opera *Madame Butterfly,* an opera in which I reveled during my eleven years of childhood in Europe, often expressed how this musical writing was channeled to him in a vision from God. Had Puccini ignored this flash of inspiration to a hallucination, we would not have this musical performance extraordinaire for our public feasting. The metacosmic voids left if these inspirations, whether visual, auditory, kinesthetic or mental, were left unacknowledged would be beyond our comprehension.

Quantum spirituality provides you many bits and pieces as possibilities for your spirituality. It points you to the infinite potential inherent in you and celebrates your journey, which is no longer a mystery but supported by quantum physics. You are a re-creative and re-generative force stemming from the abstract Consciousness. Quantum spirituality will be your rocket booster.

Orthodoxy has failed you and has failed many people. Orthodoxy is the opiate of the masses! Defange orthodoxy and tell them you will no longer continue to see life through a narrow band. Orthodoxy has been the greatest hoax imposed upon mankind and you need to strip the ugly machination behind orthodoxy. The universe will breathe more freely when it dissolves. Do not get caught up over the authority of a whole cloth because it is dangerous to allow such cultist control. The victims of such authority continue to live in the shadows until there is an awakening and start listening to their inner voice. You are strangled by the ugly cord of salvation which has made a fearful helpless slave of you. You will hemorrhage if you stay in this fear. The rote system of orthodoxy does not allow you to sustain nor originate constructive thinking and ideas. It has been a hollow mockery which you have accepted prima facie and has enmeshed you in the coils of numerous false suppositions.

On the other hand, quantum spirituality sees you as a finite-infinite being with endless potential and endless possibilities. It is empowering because it provides you more than one path for your evolution. Yet most of you walk in ignorance of all of this and are blinded to the Kingdom of Heaven within. Stop listening to the words of false minions and listen to what calls to you from within. Otherwise, you are going to become your own betrayer. You cannot be to anyone else anymore than you allow yourself to be. Through quantum spirituality you will fly like a homing dove to the Home of the Father of Light. Through silence will erupt a flood of creative information, and you will begin to feel and see the expression of Infinite Creative Source. Living the quantum life will catalyze your transformation. However, "wisdom arises through effort," as the Buddha said.

Orthodoxy teaches you slavery which comes from false leadership. Quantum spirituality teaches you self-emancipation. Find your immortal heritage, not by seeing through the eyes of another person, who in most cases is as blind as you are, but by going into the Silence Within. You will not find your true expression by listening to the outward expression of psychotic mass subjugation. You will only find it by going into your inner silence. You possess the power of selection and discrimination beyond the circumstances of orthodoxy in which you have been raised. Quantum spirituality is your road map. Go inward. Go into your silence and connect with your Sourceness. Source is pure energy and you have been given many sparks of it already which contain many points of realization.

THE GODLESS FICTION
OF OUR LIVES

To be modest in speaking truth is hypocrisy
Kahlih Gibran

This world is a dangerous hallucination. You are filled with propaganda that has turned you into a programmed sheep. Normal is not healthy. Normal is not joyous. It is merely what the masses are doing and the masses are neurotic in their groveling submission to authority. The masses are form-imprisoned spirits. What orthodoxy has been telling you is happening is what you are believing is happening. This has been destroying you because you have been blinded to the Truth of who you are because of the web of lies you have been fed. You have been fed junk and have not been nourished. You have been fed misleading information and ancient wisdom has been suppressed. You are living a delusional tale. Orthodoxy has kept you in the stone-age. Orthodoxy is a highly weaponized media and has been cannibalizing your soul. Live in harmony with the land of your soul and be sustainable by starting a dynamic inquiry through your quantum field with your soul. Follow the heart not the crowd.

The adjusted individual does not exercise an independence of opinion but a universal uniformity to assimilate into the masses! You are so bound to this dumb conformity built from deceptive tricks that you hardly perceive your bonds. Orthodoxy protects the foundation of falsehood. They guard the unreal world. You have been turned into a crawling insect, when you are actually in the ascent to the Divine. You are lost in a crowd and drowning in a consciousness of conformity and contradictions. How long do you want to continue to bend your knee to convention? How long do you want to stay in this material trance? How long will you quell your self-mastery for the faceless masked ranks of mass society? You spend most of your life believing all you were told as the real deal, then one day you wake up and find out it was all a lie.

You feel your emptiness and discontent. It comes from your conformity that has caused your gifts to be locked inside when you want to express yourself fully and be a creative being. Break off from herd mentality or you will squander away having lived someone else's life rather than your own. A wider application of understanding must be achieved. If you do not change, you will continue to crawl with the turkeys rather than fly with the eagles! Do you dare walk away from the enmeshment of this old model, or do you have too much at stake to walk away and never look back, even though you know it has caused you to forget the infinite Light being that you are and does not serve you well? You know that it is an irresponsible system that infantilizes you. When you accept something, it holds you in place. Have you made a good bargain — conformed respectability (herd mentality) versus loss of individuality (nonconformist). Would you regret the former more than you regret the latter? Can you really continue to stand in silence against the exploitation and harvesting of souls that is happening today in our world without your emotions going into outrage? By negating conformity and herd mentality, you negate the discord. By negating the disorder of orthodoxy and in society, you are negating the discord within yourself. Now there is silence. That is the beginning of the change.

You are living in an invisible straightjacket by not questioning the assumptions upon which you have built your life. These are not irreversible setbacks, however. You can take various actions to connect with Consciousness for a greater purpose. Is it time for you to be more expanded in your awareness? There is a better way to live!

Many of you carry anxiety and toxic shame to your very roots. You keep yourself in a slavery so that your life is not yours by following social mores which are not moral. I am not suggesting licentious freedom, because freedom requires tremendous discipline. Yet it has been dangerous and deadly to have spent your entire life looking for Source through the light of someone else rather than your own inner light. I am talking about the freedom from letting go of all suppression so you can see things very clearly and every decision you make is in the best interest of all concerned. No, you cannot not choose, because by factor of not making a choice you are choosing a particular way of being. Whatever choice you make will affect all other choices which you make in your life.

There is some level of comfort in your imprisonment isn't there because others are making decisions for you. But if you unslave yourself from orthodoxy and rise in consciousness, now you have to start making your own decisions. Orthodoxy is providing you an escape from personal responsibility. By keeping yourself enslaved and denying yourself your individual freedom, you are also denying yourself your spiritual evolution. Orthodoxy and social conventions are doing you much more damage than you realize because this conditioning is not superficial. Years of propaganda through repetition and ritual have influenced and conditioned your mind. The conditioning goes very deep by placing on us all the labels that divide us. All these labels that create division also create fear. We are divided by nationalities, by languages, by religions, by color, by political parties. Yet what is more critical to realize is that this society has developed from our collective psychological state. Society is a sad reflection of all of our fears, aggressions and brutality. The change must start from within each one of us individually if we are going to make changes in our society. What we are we have made the world. Therefore, the problems in the world are not outward, but inward. We are caught in a trap that we built for ourselves. This is serious and intense. Yet if we are going to flip this enormity of misery, what is required is for each one of us to learn to live a totally different life by becoming extraordinarily awake in order to begin to live at peace with ourselves. Start by never following another because you have become a second-hand person. It is frightening, isn't it, to be alone with oneself without having an emotional meltdown or becoming neurotic. There are no saviors out there including the author. Look within! There is a better way to live!

Individual effort is mandatory for your evolution. You have been conditioned to follow. Without individual effort and awareness, you lack meaning and significance. Effort gives it meaning. Through this effort is how you find your bliss. Accept personal responsibility for your evolution, and you will find your strength. Drop your present limitations so you can rise into another level of consciousness. Be the teacher and disciple of yourself because no one can lift you to the next step-up except yourself. Out of your struggles, something new will evolve. Have a meditative mind and with clear eyes and unconditioned, seek that which is more than transient, something beyond propaganda. Once you open this door, you will find out for yourself what is sacred.

You have even turned sex into a surface encounter because of all the anxiety created around sexual activity. This is the age of "instamacy" as a very bright physician client recently commented! Some of you have taken orthodoxy into your bedrooms and triangulated yourself. The rest use love merely as a lure for the sex act. It has become the foreplay for the act and the act of sex is nothing more than using another for the release of physical pleasure. It is also a way that you are looking for yourself through someone else. There is nothing wrong in that, but see it for what it is. Artificial. You were born and harvested in artificiality, and you keep yourself there. You have become drugged and drunk on artificial sex! Partners have become replaceable like automobile parts. You have forgotten the sacredness of sexuality. You have killed the spiritual side of it because so many have made it their primary outlet for their life's energy. It will never deepen love because love is talking and meditative. I believe that all couples would benefit from attending a workshop in eastern tantric sex which is totally misunderstood and perceived as some exotic frantic love-making. Three of the premises of tantric sex is that men hold, more often than not, their ejaculations during intercourse, which restores their vital energy; that the couple breathe together and circulate that energy around their hearts and up and down the chakras as one whole; and let lovemaking become a relaxed meditative experience without any performance goals. It is an intense form of intimacy and communion that transforms.

There can be no love as long as there is an expectation to get something back from the other person. That is not love but mere exchange of bodily fluids. This is merely bondage. When you participate in sexual activity consciously, however, it becomes a meditative sacred experience and you learn to be sufficient onto yourself. Conscious responsibility on the part of both partners is required if sex is to become spiritually meaningful. A moment of total nakedness. However, in society, sex is compulsive and perverted for many with hit and run sex. It is a sport rather than a sacred act. It becomes a slavery because you cannot live without it. Sexual addictions are rampant in our society. This makes sex a daily routine and becomes boring and no longer satisfying. You are left unfulfilled. Sexuality has become neurotic like most things in society today because it has become either repressed or exploited.

When sex becomes more than just a release from tension, rather than one partner being as good as another, and it becomes more a state of mind and a true expression of love, then you will feel fulfilled because it will be celebrated. Through the conscious act of sex, which is the most sacred and deep act with nature, you can move to the divine and eventually you will naturally transcend sex. No sublimation, just pure spontaneous transcendence. Dualities moving into union and dissolving into blissful oneness. You will move from doing to being. No goal, just the present moment. What most are seeking in sex is bliss and as you mature in consciousness, this bliss will go upward into the spiritual chakras and sex becomes irrelevant because now you have true not temporary bliss. Create a sacred space for your love-making. Breathe together, make love slowly and merge together joyfully. Develop body awareness so you can be completely receptive to your body. Your body is the Temple of Spirit. Develop a healthy respect for your genitalia. Explore them so you can develop a sacred connection to these very sacred parts of your body. Consider the vagina as the gate to the divine, and the penis as the key to open the gate to the divine. In sex you are tapping on your kundalini center, original source of life, in the muladhara root chakra. Together you open the divine door. It is a merger amongst man, woman and nature!

It is meditative when you enter into your sexuality with full consciousness. Go deep into it and experience the inner intercourse. In physical sex, bodies meet; in spiritual sex, souls meet. It becomes a conscious meeting between you and Source. Transcend your physical body and become the Source. No duality. There is not an act more powerful than the act of sex. Without the act of sex, you and I would not be having this dialogue. Seek your Oneness through sex and it will never master you; you will transcend the physical act into a spiritual union and you will evolve into a maturity of wholeness. Start your adventure with full awareness and a friendly attitude and see where it takes you. Turn on the Light in the darkness of your night so you can see the Divine all around you. Once you see the stars from under the sky, you will see how limiting it was to look through the windows. Do not go back to looking through the windows. You need to grow under the open sky like a tree in all directions.

BECOME A TRUSTEE
OF YOUR SOUL

W hat you have been taught does not represent the fundamental truth of things. It is not even sustainable without your spiritual life becoming very costly. Is what you learned what you want to pass on to your children or is there a better way for them to live? Can you give your children your history without taking away their future of Infinite Intelligence? You need to inspire them with a real purpose in life not ties to corporate and orthodox lines. Do you want to be the trustee of your soul and teach your children the same, or will you just let anybody invest in it with your permission?

No longer offer your soul to your perpetrators. Climb the ladder of Spirit instead. Search for your Oneness from within. Stop chasing after others to help you to escape. Open up your voice chakra and say loudly to yourself, "I will no longer accept that way of thinking!" Do not any longer be satisfied with the limitations because the quantum vacuum which provides infinite possibilities is enormous! Orthodoxy has been a supreme exercise in futility. Abandon orthodoxy. When Krishna in the <u>Bhagavad Gita</u> attempted to persuade Arjuna to battle and abandon his family and teachers, this was metaphorical for abandoning orthodoxy and going inward.

What *are* you teaching your children? You know that you cannot teach your children anything that you yourself do not have and you have only what you believe. So, choose well your future husband or your future wife. Choose with great discretion because your children will inherit the qualities of their parents. Find a partner who has an unconditioned consciousness, a partner who is awake. A partner who is fully aware that her/his world is his conditioned consciousness objectified. One's world is a mirror of self. By looking at a potential partner's world, you can determine the state of consciousness in which a potential partner lives. In order to find a partner who is awake, *you* must awaken first because in life you attract what you are not what you want! You cannot *give* any of this to your children; you can only resurrect that which lies asleep within them.

Perhaps this is a good time to sit for a moment in silence and *feel* what it is like to have already achieved that which you now recognize to be true of yourself, awakened, unconditioned. Just momentarily focus on the end goal and not worry about the means of how you will get there. Just for a moment wear the *mood* of being totally free from orthodoxy and convention. *Feel* what it is like to be awake! Let go of the shackles. Feel the freedom. Feel the joy of having realized your end goal. Feel the bliss. Feel, feel, feel! When you can feel your end goal and the life that follows as a result of it, the Universe will come around to support you in fully realizing this invisible state into your day-to-day reality if you stay long enough in this fixed attitude of mind. Nothing will be able to stop it from embodying itself. Believe what is denied perhaps by your senses. You must be your highest ideal. What you cannot envision as being Source, you cannot put upon yourself because you and Source are ONE. What you believe you are, God is. I AM a fifth dimensional being!

What are the universities teaching your children? "One quarter of the professors in universities call themselves Marxists or socialists to remake this society into something it is not. Universities are radical boot camps for radical ideas not the Truth. They have their eyes closed. They are unaware and asleep. Most, not all, have no real concern for your children but only in how anything promotes them and their investment portfolio. Higher education does not explore Truth. It does not develop ideas. It is merely poisoning your children. You really need to decide whether you want your hard-earned money to keep funding radicalism through your tuitions because a false reality is being fed to them every day" according to Dr. Tim Groseclose, Economics Professor at the George Mason University, Adam Smith Chair at the Mercatus Center, and Dr. John Ellis who is Chairman of the Association of Scholars and Distinguished Professor Emeritus of German Literature at the University of California, Santa Cruz. Universities are "clear indoctrination of our youth" they warned on a program I viewed recently on television! They have become "places of rebellion." I will venture to say that the majority of the large universities will become the dinosaurs of the future. The diploma might as well be a parrot's beak because graduates are programmed to think and speak the same unless they awaken quickly upon graduation as some do. The latter, who dare to speak differently from the rigid academic teachings laid out during their tenure, are often punished. They get targeted and black-listed. Sounds pretty medieval to me.

Despite the fact that I acquired two doctorates, one in psychology and one in quantum advanced medicine, and am an earnest highly motivated learner, I never resonated with conventional education. I recall as a very early elementary student in a convent school in Malta, Europe where I was born and raised, the many mornings I subjected my mother to my screaming tantrums and sobbing because I refused to go to school. The mere thought of going to school seriously traumatized me. It would reach unmanageable levels so that eventually my mother, exhausted and helpless, would call for the police to take me into school. The uniformed police would get me to the school, at which point I would huddle into a corner of the building unwilling to stay in the classroom. I have very little memory of subsequent years in junior high, and by then we had moved to America, except that I was double promoted and skipped from fifth to the seventh grade. Perhaps at some subconscious level I may have made the decision to excel so I can expedite exiting such institutions. In high school in America, I feigned illnesses numerous times in order to be kept home or to be dismissed early from school and sent home. Even as a child I was already experiencing the bondage that comes from orthodox institutions. A child's early intuition, perhaps, about the damage that was about to be done and was being done. In college I completed twenty-seven credit hours in one semester with special dispensation from the Dean since I was very strong academically. All I wanted was out! I love to learn. I find conventional schools intolerable to my soul.

You, yourself, need to teach your children who are on loan to you in a custodial undertaking, the Truth of how to be the caretakers of their souls. In order to be able to do that, you need to learn to manage your own power. You cannot teach what you do not know. You yourself need to leave behind your illusions so you can find your soul because for centuries you have allowed orthodoxy to imprison you. You yourself need to redefine your view of what it is to live and who you are. Now awaken! *You* are the only one for whom you are waiting. There is no one else.

Be the CEO and guardian of your soul because orthodoxy food is deplete of the nutrients necessary for your spiritual evolution. Orthodoxy lacks real power to move your soul because it rarely satisfies. It is not providing you the spiritual nutrients essential for your growth. This propaganda is a boomerang because the world you create for yourself will either be a gift or a curse that will come right back at you.

This life has failed to satisfy. Look toward Consciousness for harmony. Look only toward yourself for your salvation because there is no external person or process who can save you. Your individual self is really Infinite Consciousness. Your Consciousness has the necessary elements. These elements come from your organic soulic gardening and cannot come from an outside source full of pesticides. Do not allow logic and reason to replace Infinite Intelligence. You need to allow the downward causation model which begins with Consciousness to inform you first with additional understandings which initially may come from reason. You must initiate the creation of your own reality.

There is no blueprint; nor is there a fixed plan. All that is necessary is for you to start a transition initiative for your evolution and for the greater good of all. Meditation is your vehicle for multi-output and to live the quantum life. It is a natural remedy that resonates with our Original Self.

Meditation is a technology that no one can control, manipulate or bastardize. It does not chemicalize you nor radiate you. Meditation fasts your monkey-mind. Meditation creates an environment for you in which to blossom because it is the Great Teacher. It will help you to become, not just capable, but sensible. Understand, that in order for you to absorb the malevolent manipulation of orthodoxy, you have to be at the same vibrational state and frequency range. For you to absorb the fear orthodoxy generates, you have to be there also. When your frequency is higher, as through meditation, low vibration passes through you. It will not be able to connect with you. That is why in life you attract what you are not what you want. You attract that of the same vibrational state.

You cannot grow without removing the old. Harmony is a much higher frequency. Orthodoxy does not want harmony but disharmony. Orthodoxy creates disharmony through fear, shame and guilt. However, with harmony you switch off their electricity. They can no longer control you. This is orthodoxy's greatest fear that you will stop being a slave to their system and stop adhering to their limitations. As Buddha himself discovered that the beginning of liberation is the ending of conditioning. You do not realize the extent to which you have become conditioned. Do not conform. Stop composing the same music your predecessors composed. Find your own music. Once you make this decision you will find your freedom! Your freedom must always include the best interest of all concerned. Freedom must be dedicated to the Supreme Ideal. Anything short of that is not spirituality, it is utter selfishness. Your motivation must come from the transcendental dimension of recombination of child and elder simultaneously. In order to honor the immaculate state of your core, however, you do not need to become self-righteous. Sanctimony is most boring! Be childlike. Lean more toward the humor of the child! Do you dare have your own power? If so, then start your spiritual housecleaning. Plenty of dust has accumulated, and it cannot be cleaned out only once. It requires your full attention.

Man created the anthropomorphic God. God did not create man. There is no man/God sitting on a throne watching you under a microscope ready to judge you. There is only you! Big hoax you have been fed and by continuing to allow this hoax, you are endorsing. By endorsing you become! If you continue to put your faith in anything but yourself, you will destroy yourself.

God and man are the same. Man is a stepped-down vibrational God. You are Infinite Creative Intelligence – that deep core of energy within you that guides and enlightens your every move. God is the Ocean of Consciousness. You are Source. You are God. "You are the world," Krishnamurti, a world teacher, advised, and he stressed the need for an inner revolution. You are a wave in that Ocean of Consciousness. There is only the "I AM". No matter how far away you walk with a handful of water from the Ocean, that wave is still the same chemical compound as the Ocean. You cannot destroy its essence. It is an impossibility. The wave itself is impermanent because eventually it must merge into the Ocean. Therefore, it is impossible to "sin" against Infinite Creative Intelligence, the Ocean. This is simply preposterous. You were not born in "original sin". You were born in original Truth. You were born in Spirit! You were not born soiled. You were born purified. You can never change your essence because your essence is Divinity. There is nothing that can change the quality of the soul. These are tales told to you all to control the masses and create a wall of mental darkness. These tales have disconnected you from your interdimensional spiritual identity. When you "sin" you have forgotten your true identity and have gotten absorbed only in your material world of self-imprisoned narrowness. Therefore, there was no "original sin". There was only original forgetting of who you are. There is no heaven or hell up there or down there. Heaven and hell are states of consciousness in which you live. Expand your vision because there is no one to change but yourself. You will see this truth when you reach your deeper and larger consciousness after you awaken out of your sleep. Drop into the Ocean of Consciousness so that the drop becomes the wave and the wave is lost into the Ocean.

Equally as preposterous is that someone outside yourself can save you from your "sins" like a confessor or spiritual healer or Master. This is pure hypocrisy that has been perpetuated on you by orthodoxy. If you continue with this unrealistic attitude you will destroy your spirituality. The Master Confessor is living, breathing and regenerating within you. Nowhere else. There is no one else! There is only you! Clarity of your soul must take place from within you and not from an exterior superficial force. Do not look for your healing in the church, the universities or in the hospital. Your healing must start from the inside out not the outside in. No longer hold on to these myopic views held by mass consciousness. Note that orthodoxy does not have an investment in supporting this new thinking because it diminishes their control. Most of your orthodox leaders to whom you have given away your powers are more oriented toward politics than they are toward your soul and health. Let go of so much of your false hysterical reverence. Become Self-conscious in a way that reclaims your power because your orthodox conventional leaders are themselves not conscious enough to help your emergence. You created yourself to learn about Self. You can choose to work with one spoke or use your entire wheel. You are a free being. Make your choice.

FEAR IS NEVER A PRIVATE AFFAIR

The greatest strength is gentleness
Iroquois

Fear is a great control mechanism and has costly consequences. It is a weapon of coercion to get someone to do its bidding. Fear is an energy current in your body and has many side effects. It locks your mind. It is insidious and very tenacious and cuts you off from Source. It is the base operating system of organizational orthodoxy. It wastes useful energy and is the cause of significant impairment. Jesus constantly reminded us, "Fear not, be not afraid." Furthermore, anything that is predicated by fear and patriarchal domination should be avoided. If you feel threatened you will have a nagging concern to secure yourself because you will feel in a constant state of existential alienation. This will close your heart and you will have little interest in another except as that person might threaten or promote your own end. When you get under the imperious influence of fear, it becomes very difficult for you to see others in their own right because you become like a ball of string, you cannot disentangle yourself. So your fear is never a private affair because your overriding goal is to keep your emotional economy undisturbed. You resonate your pain throughout the entire universe as you turn upon yourself creating an illusion of separateness and dualism resulting in a prison of individuality and preventing you from wholeness.

We have an inner–beingness that connects us all but through fear your field of awareness becomes significantly narrowed. You will include in your awareness only what relates to your emotional needs. Everything else is excluded. You need to develop an inner tolerance for the essence and uniqueness of others. You are forgetting your greatness because you are sleeping imprisoned. You are forgetting to turn on the Light! You are distorted and dogmatized. As the movie Matrix informed us, "You are being vampired!"

When you live in fear, your biochemistry becomes unbalanced resulting in distorted viewing because you see with your moods. Therefore, you step-down your vibratory level and create tension in every relationship because fear is reflected outwards into interpersonal relationships. Fear, therefore, is regressive and degenerative. A person in fear drives himself into a spiritual vacuum. Do not dance with fear. Dance with love, a companion of Light! Stop being afraid and wake up! Love is the absence of fear. Where love exists fear cannot. Love inspires, fear discourages. Automatons cannot love. They merely exchange personality packages and hope for a fair bargain because they are stuck in quicksand. On the other hand, love is an interdimensional bridge and an action in the mood of eternity. Love is not an exceptional-individual phenomenon. It is an unconfined frequency of energy accessible to everyone in the midst of every experience. Yet, growing into understanding takes time. It is a gradual awakening. You decide if you want to believe in fear, however, more than you want to believe in Infinite Intelligence. I prefer to let the Divine guide my choices.

When you "miss the mark" by transitioning into a low vibrational state, you will experience unbearable soulic agony (hell), because you distance yourself from your divine nature, but you cannot destroy your divine nature. When you "miss the mark" you move from the dual phenomenon of Knowledge to Ignorance, from Light to Darkness. You either move yourself closer or farther away from your Divinity by your thoughts and your behaviors. When you move farther away by misconduct, you lower your vibration, and it is no longer a good fit. You will resonate less with Infinite Creative Intelligence, the electromagnetic flux field of the universe. You become dim like a 25-watt bulb unable to shine light onto your environment. Through purity of thought, meditation and honest behavior, you raise your vibrational state, and shine like a 300-watt bulb illuminating everything around you and re-integrating with Spirit. This is your state of ecstasy (heaven) and integration with

Source. These are gems, not pebbles, so don't throw them away merely to continue with your destructive ways or you will hit rock bottom. Develop a more refined perception of spiritual matters by letting go of polarities. Then you will automatically move into your heart and away from fear.

If you cannot quite see it at this time, no worries. Just let your heart lead you. It will take you in the right direction. Do not be afraid to ask for support from Infinite Intelligence, the God-Source. The important point is that you take a step, any step, toward your goal to increase your Light body. To enhance your Light body, you must shed all your illusions. I am not saying this is easy, I am saying this is necessary, to shift from man to spiritual to supramental Being.

Meditation is a good starting point because it will help raise your frequency from 85 hertz (lowest scale) to 1000 hertz (highest scale) and that of an Enlightened Being like Babaji, Jesus, Buddha, Krishna, St. Francis, Kabir, etc. Meditation harmonizes your intention and moves you into a quantum life by bringing your mind home. It connects breath with your life force and helps you to realize your body as light. Through meditation you can access the full range of healing abilities.

Meditation will end the many waves of deluded thoughts. What will you do when you shed all your illusions? Then you will make choices from an awakened state. You will choose consciously what is truly aligned with your soul. You will stop tithing to be controlled. You will unlock the tether of your fear and start your transformation which will happen within your human frequency and not necessarily in your external environment. Although, it will not be unusual that you will begin to gravitate toward individuals who are more in your frequency range or even higher and who are better aligned with your evolved choices. Note that everyone who comes into your life comes to teach you something about yourself. When you reach a particular vibration, specific individuals come into your life so you can receive input from these lives about who you are and where you are. Then remember that your brother is yourself. Before I begin any therapeutic session with my clients, I always state inwardly, *"Blessed and Divine Father, please give me a listening heart"*. Then I ask myself, *"Why has Spirit come into my office in this body?"* knowing that every person is myself wearing a different body.

WHEN YOU MISS THE MARK

However, what would happen to you if in this earth-life you become significantly destructively inclined, an incorrigible and a criminal of the world? You will interfere with the equilibrium of your life because you rape yourself energetically. However, your center remains the same.

Someone who has become destructively inclined disrupts his frequency patterns and relationships of his energy patterns. Such a person, rather than expanding his energy system, condenses it. He will become increasingly compressed and then degenerates because he will lack spiritual aeration. This is not a weak person; just someone who has not become fully integrated. This is someone who has "missed the mark", because he continues to live a life of limitations. You need to eliminate from your consciousness, the duality of good and evil, however, which implies a judgment, and replace those words with the realistic concepts of quantum physics of positive and negative energy wave forms because even in our brokenness there is the Divine.

This partial knowledge you call "evilness" disrupts frequency patterns of energy and interferes with the progressive development of superconsciousness. "Evilness" is the expression of negative polarity with the more positive biased Infinite Intelligence. It is spiritual suicide. You move from Knowledge to Ignorance and you suffer because you contract yourself. Therefore, you will not be able to temporarily absorb spiritual energies directly into your psychic body. It is similar to having pneumonia and becoming incapable of taking in oxygen freely into your lungs. The air is always there, but you are incapable of drawing it in because you have constricted your lungs. In the spiritual worlds, you will be unable to "breathe" spiritual oxygen until you make some changes compatible with the necessary frequency for breathing in spiritual energy. You have spiritual pneumonia and will be more miserable than you were once before.

Good and evil are shifting quantities, however, and our evolution is progressive which means it is also shifting. Furthermore, how can you put limitations on the Infinite by rigid standards of conduct. We need to keep taking action toward higher consciousness as led by the Supreme Light and evaluate all standards as we progress. Your spiritual development is inclusive of falls since in the falling there is learning. Even the incorrigibles will become Creators. Therefore, Hitler is as important as Jesus in the eyes of Infinite Intelligence because he is only expressing for the moment. "Is a diamond less valuable because it is covered with mud? God sees the changeless beauty of our souls. He knows we are not our mistakes," Paramahansa Yogananda.

Get rid of your fanaticism and move toward openness because the divine resides in everyone, and we are all stumbling creatures. Good and evil are primitive thoughts from primeval causes and are misunderstood. They are a movement of Infinity. Destroying such illusions of good and evil will be a most important step in your own spiritual development. Do not compromise your honor for small things. Do not compromise your spirit. Without spirit you have nothing! Meditate and utilize this technology of multidimensional attention. Decide which is constructive or which is destructive toward your evolutionary pattern. Everyone learns of Infinite Intelligence in his own way. Do not miss the mark, hit the mark!

Since everything is a movement of Consciousness, the Absolute Force, a dynamic system that is constantly changing, you can turn around this compression and degeneration of consciousness by constructing a positive force of action to oppose your previous destructive act. In other words, no act is a final act. Just as life is infinite, so is redemption, and it will lead to greater transcendence. In the spirit world, the door is always open to reformation. Furthermore, since everything is ONE, there has to be some sense of unity even in what we may perceive as "evil" because nothing can be a mere mistake of Infinite Intelligence lacking in meaning or divine wisdom. Infinite Creative Intelligence executes infallibly.

Your "Father within" continues to guide you through your spiritual dance of life. When you inner listen, you will move from being a passive vessel to a living spring, from being a parasite upon life to becoming a patron of life through your interrelatedness. Furthermore, through the pure experience of the quantum you are never restricted to two possibilities. You have a superposition of possibilities from which to evolve yourself. It is never either this or that but an entirely new coherent superposition of your true Self in which you will experience the all-pervading unity. Through this interrelatedness everything you do, therefore, you do to yourself!

It is your mind which creates your hell and your heaven. It is your thoughts which take you there. You have imposed the external devil upon yourself through your ignorance because you have lived on the opinion of others so far. The shadow resides within each one of us through our thinking. You can create the devil or divinity within your own mind as you wish. With every thought you have, you either increase or decrease your vibration. Every thought you think is a reflection of your spirit, your higher frequency. Everything you think, therefore, has a cosmic significance.

Your senses are stepped-down vibrational sources of supply for the content of your spirit mind. However, when you dim your light by "missing the mark" through negative thinking or behaviors, you never dim the Original Light, any more than you dim the light of an original candle from which you light numerous other candles. You can make or unmake yourself with your thoughts and dim your light and lower your vibration, step down the ladder, but you cannot "sin" against Spirit. Sin, therefore, is not a part of Consciousness. Sin is you hurting your own self-expression (descending). Your consciousness of "sin" is what has driven you to find salvation in orthodoxy. Orthodoxy is full of fears – fear of God lest you will be punished, fear by the torments of hell lest you burn forever, fear of death and perishability, fear of sin that creates guilt and shame to keep you imprisoned, fear of living so that you mortify the flesh instead of honoring it as the temple of Spirit!

Goodness, on the other hand, is you ennobling your self-expression (ascending). Goodness is being in the service of others. Goodness is acting in the best interest of all concerned. Goodness always has with it an altruistic component. A thought is all that is needed to cause you to fall back or to convert your frequency! All is a stage in your evolution. A thought, therefore, is like a seed. It produces whatever you plant. If you plant a corn seed for sure you will not grow a banana! So be careful what you plant into the fertile soil of your consciousness. No outer change is ever possible without first an inner revolution. The circumstances of your life are connected to what is happening in your internal world. So look out of this world literally and think fourth and fifth dimensionally.

There is always a Superior Pressure from Consciousness nudging you to climb the ladder of Spirit. Through the continuous dance of the descent of Consciousness into matter and the ascent of matter into Consciousness, you can recover your Infinity and your Divine Light and live fully in your dynamic potentiality. Through this process you will become grounded in the fact that you are not flesh, but life-force condensed from the soul and mind of Infinite Creative Intelligence.

Your mind is your spirit, which lives in a higher dimension than that of your physical anatomy and brain. Amongst Spirit, Mind and Body, you have many subtle states so that your existence is a complex weft and harmony amongst your many layers. In these layers, you are constantly either climbing or descending the ladder of Spirit. The top rung of your Original Light, Consciousness, has no boundaries unlike the lowest rung of your physical body. Your top rung has greater permanence, greater potentiality and plasticity. It is a richer world at the top. You ascend to Spirit and descend to matter. Stop keeping your divinity a secret any longer.

There is a price to be paid for every step-up you take in consciousness, however. You cannot become more sensitive to life by being more positively charged without becoming more sensitive to pain and danger. This susceptibility is soil for further spiritual growth. As your frequency increases you will develop less and less interest in the finite, physical and what the material world has to offer. You will know that your heart and soul are not made for the finite but for the Infinite. This discontent, while in the third dimensional world, is the sign and seal of your infinity and divinity.

CONNECTING WITH
YOUR INNER SOURCE

The core of your life is spiritual. You return to earth repeatedly in order to bring yourself into better alignment with Infinite Intelligence. This is the perennial philosophy of your existence. Through your understanding of quantum spirituality and through meditation, which invite and encompass every aspect of life, you will be able to access truths to your consciousness and convert them into action. Then you will connect with your inner Self and your true identify. Quantum spirituality takes you back to the Source. This is the grand design of life toward your spiritual transformation.

Had I not trusted this alignment with my Infinite Intelligence I would not have facilitated the healing of a woman who came into my office for therapy. I was seeing Michelle, an Afro-American woman, for the first time. As she walked into my office, I saw a bouncing theatrical animated cartoon-like figure of Casper bouncing on her right shoulder that identified himself to me as a boy by coming in on the right, the masculine side. Michelle felt blocked in most areas of her life but was very vague as to the cause. When I questioned whether her issues had anything to do with the male baby figure bouncing on her right shoulder, she sobbed profusely, barely able to utter amidst her tears, "It was a boy then!" Amidst drenching tears cascading down her cheeks, she related the events, unprompted, which led to her abortion at a very young age for which she carried guilt and shame that blocked her life's energy. She had been in years of treatment unsuccessfully and had become a recluse. That one session released her from further therapy.

I explained to Michelle that abortions, along with the presumptuous bravado of judgments which come with abortions from others, might in some circumstances, delay the re-integration of an individual's circuitry because the cultural judgments instill fear and toxic shame. The secret this woman kept continued to gain power through the years. Furthermore, the anticipated judgments increase darkness. These judgments are not a part in which Source would participate. Abortions are by no means a failure.

Stop living in a glass house. Such decisions need to be left to the mother and the child. It is a unified conjoint decision be assured. It is their evolution, not yours. Don't meddle even by thought. Furthermore, the soul of the unborn baby must have been in agreement or it would not have happened at all. No one leaves the body until the soul wills it. No force other than Source exists. This force is Self.

For the mother who experienced an abortion, a focus of her healing to get herself out of fear and shame is to channel Light through her upper chakras. The heart, throat, third eye, and crown chakras might be the points of consideration for increasing the vibratory power lost through fear and guilt and will facilitate expeditiously the mother's growth. This allows the soul to connect with its divine activity and fuse with Source once more. One needs to become still enough and listen within. Then the mother might anchor herself in the heart/thymus chakra to fully access her Light body again.

Some wonder at which point a soul enters a fetus? Is it at conception or is it at birth? Is there a consciousness behind the form? I remember reading an article somewhere many years ago how President John F. Kennedy was faced with these moral questions when his administration experimented with a human body produced, without female embodiment, in a laboratory, and raised it in an atmosphere of nitrogen for space missions. Did this test tube baby have a soul? Did a soul join such a body at its discretion merely because it may want to have such an experience? High probability I tend to think, because I believe that body and soul fuse at a unitary moment. I also believe the soul has a choice to delay its fusion with the body. I believe free will enters into all our decisions. A soul would have to enter a body in order for physicality to have a consciousness according to quantum spirituality.

Do not underestimate the damage we do when either gender

experiences an energy abortion. This is the aborting of creative energies toward a creative project or pursuit. Energy abortions can cause as many scars as fetal abortions and throw your second chakra off balance. When you do not give birth to an idea or project and continue to carry this death in your cellular system, you block the energy of the second chakra resulting in potential uterine or prostate problems for example.

Which connects me to another point related to miscarriages. Miscarriages often are babies who are eager to come in from a high spiritual level and attempt to connect on the physical. Their high intensity burns up the fragile physical body and the soul re-integrates into Source. Often this is attempted several times until the new spirit learns to regulate its high energy power through its chakras from the spirit side. Sometimes these babies burn themselves up in matter of hours or days, and thus the initial delay of a menstrual cycle, and then its reappearance. The child takes too big of a leap in its attempt to bring in its energy and doesn't relate to it well enough to manage it. It is like taking a giant leap onto a trampoline and missing the trampoline. For that child it is not the right time.

Begin to go inward so you can find out what is true for you and then you can become self-reliant because up to now you have built your life on the ideas of others. Go into your Silence in order to ascend from Darkness to Light and from Ignorance to Knowledge. Meditate because it is the biggest gift you can give yourself. Think again who you are and for what purpose you are here. Through meditation you will find your true Self because you will break from the way you "normally" lived your life in orthodoxy. Normal merely means you are a part of the consistent pattern. The consistent pattern in our society is neurotic. It does not mean healthy. Do not define yourself by orthodox normal culture. You are Integrated Unlimitedness.

You are divine potentiality and possibilities. Stop your fear and desperation. Be bold and edgy. Stop running. Stop hiding behind answers in conventional patterns. The conventional model is an irresponsible model because it has stripped you of your own thinking.

You are quantum and electromagnetic. You are both continuous and discontinuous. You are both linear and nonlinear. You are finite and you are infinite. You are an expression of the reality of Consciousness which is Infinite with manifold finiteness.

Your creative capacity is so much greater than what you think is possible. You are powerful beyond belief! A shift in attitude and consciousness is necessary, however, if you want to experience your true Divinity and connect with your inner Source. Wait for clarity if you do not know what to do and wait for the impulse to act. Wait for intuition to talk with you because intuition is a cosmic download that carries with it responsibilities. A shift from conditioning is essential if you want to be an authentic human.

Cleanse yourself of false perceptions, no matter how uncomfortable, in order to hear and see the message from Infinite Creative Intelligence in every moment of your life. This conditioning has kept you vibrating in the same frequency relationship which originally created the situation at birth!

The moment you were born you were tagged male or female. From there you were tracked which has limited your potentiality. After your gender was determined, from then all your acquisitions were conditioned. From there you were told what you believe. The moment you accepted the position of your gender, you followed specific tracks or disciplines accepted by your culture. You became shackled by this identification. Anchor only in your Self not your gender.

Have you ever asked yourself why you believe what you believe? Do you really believe what you believe? Or do you merely believe what has been taught to you by parents, schools, churches, society, universities or the roots of orthodox thinking which protect the unreal world. The primary capital which you have, and the only acquisition which will serve you well throughout life, is your own knowingness. Go deep into yourself, still your mind, and illuminate yourself through your vast illimitable self-vision.

Wake up to the fact that you are not doing your own thinking because these institutions have caused your extraordinary abilities to atrophy. Your insights were planted and cultivated by external sources from birth which have stunted your spiritual growth. Such propaganda has entrenched you in a prison of self-centered limitation and sterile fixations as you continue to gaze outward for direction. These heaps of conventions and habits of which society has made you, drown out your inner voice of growth by creating fixed mental patterns and a collective hypnosis which you call reality. This has been the pathological process of your life which you call reality, i.e. being manipulated from birth to death; being told who enters heaven or hell; tithing for control and to pay your way to heaven, interference in your marriage, etc. Do you dare to wake up? Do you dare to think large?

The answers are within you. There is no one outside of you. There is no there there! There is no one to judge you. Everything happens within yourself. There is only *you*. Once you allow for new thinking, you will be relieved of an incredible burden because you have been living a partial life. Your fragmentation is so deep. You are no longer alive. You are closer to death. Your tensions come from trying to fit yourself into something which has become obsolete and no longer fits, like a tight shoe that you have long out-grown. Perhaps it is time to go on an inward quest toward your own enlightenment because presently you are living someone else's dream!

Anyone who insists that there is only one way Home, is teaching you fear. This type of indiscriminate "help" is violence against Spirit. To think intelligently for yourself is the beginning of true spirituality. You have not worn the same size shoes you wore when you were two-years old. Yet you continue to squeeze yourself uncomfortably into concepts which no longer fit. The goal of existence is to *be* without conditioning because this mental norm is dramatically constricted. Your spirit cannot be built on submission. It needs to be based on confidence and inner knowledge. It is a force requiring your collaboration in the future evolution of your spirit-centered world.

When you let go of discursive chatter and plastic thoughts, you will find your soul through the energy dance of Infinite Creative Intelligence, a dance of infinite transactional fields. On the other hand, if you continue to believe in limitations, you will become that which you think about. External forces have interfered capriciously with your spiritual development because orthodoxy does not understand this new dance. So do not expect it to dance with you. The aim of this book is to de-hypnotize you and awaken you to your divinity. However, if you are going to negate your illusions, you must take full responsibilities for your experiences. You can begin by differentiating between your physical and psychic self-knowing and realize that your psychic self is infinite. It is this part of you that is a continuous traveler. The physical self is merely a vehicle for your psychic self. You as an Interdimensional Being is the hallmark of the quantum life and the foundation of quantum spirituality. With this knowledge your soul will unfold, and you will develop your spiritual consciousness. You will awaken your innermost wisdom, the source of a Higher Inspiration. You will experience a transcendence that is revolutionary, and changes will occur in your life. Your spiritual evolution depends on this understanding. The Quantum Life is about the journey of your soul, a journey that will restore choice and bring healing. You will not want to return to your previous sterile limits of ordinary physical consciousness.

You are a moving temple. Value yourself by your inner experiences and not your outer activities and trappings. Reclaim yourself with the exuberance of a conqueror. Get lost in Infinity! This journey requires a staunch determination toward your divinity. There must be no word like impossible in your vocabulary in this journey. Then you will create a major revolution in your mind because the quantum life is a better way to live! The quantum life provides uncommonly useful tools to help you reframe reality, see the shadows on the wall, and maintain the inner balance of your positive and negative voices. The Quantum Life will be your beacon of light that will help you develop an undistorted life-affirming knowledge of your Infinite capabilities in your progressive evolution.

Your mind has infinite intelligence. You can nurture it. It does not need to be restricted by conditioning and your five sensory body. This nurturing must include love, purity, candidness and absolute intellectual sincerity wrapped in humility and selflessness. You have to overcome the negative blocks caused by hypnotic conditioning which have resulted in imbalances in your life.

Awareness and analysis are just a beginning of the need to reach deeper and deeper. This cancellation process requires a constant honest evaluation of yourself and your thoughts at all times. You will need to constantly be aware how your conditioning has manipulated you. Yes, you have been manipulated and betrayed since the moment you were conceived. This has significantly narrowed your consciousness. The more your consciousness is limited, the more you can be controlled. With increased consciousness you will experience greater individuation. Yet, whenever you settle for a narrowed "normal" consciousness, you will regress and lower your vibrational energy. When you understand and embrace that you are an electromagnetic being, a series of waves, frequencies and vibrations that activate your life on all levels, you will touch the spiritual component of your very being. Becoming impersonal and objective in your analysis is a basic tenant of this expanded ability. This is not about entertainment, but about touching your spirit and accessing Consciousness in all its fullness.

YOU ARE MORE THAN A SPLIT SECOND ON THE COSMIC CLOCK

I can no longer conceive of a world that is only in design finite; a world in which the Infinite Creative Intelligence interferes capriciously with our destiny and spiritual evolution. Rather we evolve through an interdimensional regenerative life cycle. The harvests of one cycle are inherited as seeds of potentiality in the next lifetime. You will inherit limitations or liberations which you generated in your previous lifetimes.

I can no longer conceive of a God who will completely annihilate His own creation by shutting the door completely at the end of one cycle after such long continued progress and when we are just of age and becoming fit to live. Death is a shift from one dimension to another. It is merely a temporary shadow. One cycle is a staircase toward the next stage of development to lead you forward if you so wish.

Your talents and experiences develop slowly, and if you are to grow in the Infinite's image and likeness you need to experience infinite opportunities, not one brief cycle of incarnation. How absurd to create man in such magnificence only to silence him eternally after a split second of the cosmic clock! This is the biggest obscenity perpetrated against humanity! The body knows it is going to shed itself at the end of each cycle. It has a built-in program to replace it.

You can no longer dismiss the interdimensional concepts of the life cycle without revealing plain lack of scholarship and deep inquiry. The sensation of a unified transactional field fits the facts of experiential life. To think otherwise is a deprivation of logic and reason and a dangerous hallucination because these principles are inviolate. They apply to all processes of life.

43

Your world is a world of individual perception built on your memories, your fears, your anxieties and desires. A multi-life perspective is not a religious belief system but a scientific fact of predictable patterns informed by quantum physics. It is your spiritual technology for self-cultivation.

Your spiritual evolution through quantum spirituality transcends customary boundaries as you will clearly understand that the terrestrial worlds are not the only worlds that exist. There are fourth and fifth dimensional worlds in which you live that extend beyond your physical body that are not limited by time and space. Your physical or atomic body is limited to one cycle of birth and death, but your psychic subtle anatomy cannot be destroyed. Therefore, you do not die because you were never your physical body. Your psychic body is regenerative due to its fourth dimensional and spiritual nature. This regeneration could not take place if your psychic anatomy did not function from a higher dimensional energy system than your physical anatomy. They are the same energy but at different frequencies. You will understand yourself only when you look beyond your physical body. Quantum spirituality, therefore, requires you to take a giant leap forward to remove the many obstacles that have hindered your full spiritual expression so that you can let your voice ripple for decades to come. A paradigm shift is essential. Once you see it, you will wonder how you missed so much for so long.

Stop your silence about the things that matter. Find your voice. Wake up to who you really are and let new energies flow through you. The more energy that flows through you, the more transformation that will occur within you. This movement in your energy will then clear your blocks. Listen to the teacher of your inner voice. This is often called channeling. Channeling is you listening to YOU. They are inspirations from your higher Self, the vastness of yourself, allowed to flow into the consciousness of your physical self. Call on the best that is within you through this channeling which flows from a subtle Light that starts from the crown of your head into your body and into the Earth. It is a connecting rod between your higher Self and your physical self that plugs you into your expanded knowledge. When you tune into this channeling, synchronicities will line up, and you will become capable of creating way more than you could rationally expect.

The dance of spirituality is most gracefully accomplished through the vision opened to you by a fuller understanding of the interdimensional concepts of the life cycle. The highest music of this divine dance is the clarity you can achieve by understanding that you are more than just an orderly linear process. You need to dance often and well. You fear thinking for yourself because of the absurdity of your belief that somehow there is some external power responsible for your salvation who will punish you. Whenever this interdimensional dance begins to overshadow your thoughts, you expel it out of fear of the unknown and continue to bow to protocol as if in a court.

Your spirit lives through many lifetimes. Simply to assert that this is not true because it cannot be proven by third-dimensional science is an unintuitive response. As psychologists, we depend on countless phenomena for diagnostic conclusions that we cannot scientifically explain but interpret each time we administer assessment instruments. We believe we comprehend ideas by looking at numbers, blots, and marks on a page. These interpretive phenomena are accepted by the judicial system as opinions premised upon scientific knowledge that satisfy standards of evidentiary reliability. Such opinions cannot be subjected to scientific scrutiny; yet they are designated and accepted as indisputable fact.

Scientists frequently admit their inability to explain completely such phenomena as DNA, the brain and memory, as they cannot yet fathom their inner workings. Our naked eyes are incapable of visualizing infra-red and ultra-violet rays. Yet we know that these spectrums exist. Our ears are incapable of perceiving the frequency of sound available to most animals. Our ears are attuned to only a few of the sound waves that are constantly beating upon our eardrums. Very short waves and very long ones are entirely imperceptible to us. Certain birds perceive the magnetic grid of the earth and use it for migration. The same with light. Light waves of very high or very low frequency cannot be detected by our unaided eyes despite the fact that they are there all the time. An interdimensional universe is probably beyond the perception of your human capabilities but not beyond the perception of your spiritual capabilities generated through quantum life.

Similar concepts including rebirth existed in Christianity until the sixth century at which time they were banned by a special council in Constantinople under the Emperor Justinian in connection with the teachings of Father Origen. The concepts of reincarnation heredity were nearly universal in ancient and pre-industrial cultures and were the cornerstone of the great Asian Indian spiritual systems and a broad spectrum of other cultures. These ancient cultures have taught us that the harvests of one cycle, or one lifetime, are inherited as seeds of potentiality into our next lifetime. You progress through the course of many lifetimes accumulating experiences which are retained in your consciousness. You inherit limitations or liberations generated from previous lifetimes. Every lifetime has its mark upon your consciousness. Each lifetime is the child of all your former lifetimes. Your present lifetime is the parent of the lives which will follow. You are constantly meeting yourself as you process each lifetime at the causal spiritual level for the purpose of maturing your soul and developing greater spiritual coherence from each lifetime versus the spiritual and emotional anorexia of orthodoxy. This coherence is reflected in your character in your next lifetime. You are constantly breaking and forming newer patterns. Your development is not a mere product of genetic/molecular patterns but also of the successive progression of reincarnation hereditary. Energetic patterns are imprinted on your cellular physical structures with each successive reincarnation.

Dr. Ian Stevenson, the Freud of this century, psychiatrist, and Carlson Professor of Psychiatry at the University of Virginia Medical School, has published five volumes through the University of Virginia Press of case histories on children who have described memories of former lives. His cases in his files now total over 2,000. Several of his articles have been published in the Journal of Nervous and Mental Diseases (JNMO). The 165th volume of this highly reputable medical journal, dated September 1977, was almost totally devoted to Dr. Ian Stevenson's research on the rebirth philosophy.

Dr. Stevenson is regarded by his colleagues as a psychiatrist of "high integrity" and of "great intellectual ability and high professional standards who takes a most painstaking approach to collection and analysis of raw data." He became very interested in reincarnational cases with children between ages two to four because children give a "richness of obscure detail" at a time when they have "limited access to information upon which they could consciously or unconsciously build a case." Furthermore, Dr. Stevenson comments, "many of these cases lend themselves to accurate verification because most previous lives terminated only a few years prior to the present incarnation. Consequently, former parents and relatives are still alive to attest to, or contradict what the children say." Dr. Ian Stevenson concluded, "The evidence is so preponderantly in favor of reincarnation that you cannot doubt it if you have anything like an open mind."

Florida psychiatrist, Dr. Brian Weiss, M.D., graduate of Yale School of Medicine authored the book _Many Lives, Many Masters_ in 1988. I spoke directly with Dr. Weiss when he and I were presenting at the same conference on past lives. He became a believer in reincarnation when one of his own patients, under hypnosis, spontaneously accessed a past life. After the publication of his book, he was deluged with letters from many other psychiatrists who preferred to remain anonymous but who "confessed" to having been doing past life regression for decades. They will not admit this publicly because they fear the ridicule and censorship. Fifty-eight percent of two hundred twenty-eight psychiatrists who responded to a survey commented that an understanding of other dimensions and psychic phenomenon needs to become an integral part of all graduates of psychiatry. You can see that there is an evolutionary thrust even by science toward wanting and needing to understand interdimensional consciousness.

Quantum physics tells us we are omnijective, not subjective and objective. There is no separation between the physical and consciousness. We are not mature enough to handle too large a dose of this implicate order however. Yet, we can see that the evolutionary fires have begun to flicker. Let us continue with our spiritual dance around the bonfire of our lives so we can midwife our way to the next plane and together learn to survive in infinity.

Research in past life is not new. Yet the research along with the wealth of clinical cases available to us internationally takes us beyond a neutral position on reincarnation and invites investigation. Furthermore, 40 million Americans are grounded in reincarnation philosophy according to recent polls. Despite these figures, we know that truth does not stand or fall by a show of hands. An open-minded inquirer will examine ideas which may deepen his vision and lead further toward spiritual illumination. With the multitude of growing evidence available that reincarnations occur, we need to explore what value rebirth plays in our lives.

Each life, therefore, is a fragment of a long, long story with death being the end of a chapter but not the end of our story. Immortality gives you the assurance of progressive improvement. From incarnation to incarnation you transmigrate the moral and intellectual essences which shape your spirit. Your life is a proportional facsimile of your efforts in a previous lifetime.

These concepts were a fact of life until the sixth century A.D. As a matter of survival the official Christian church avoided the concept of reincarnation and would not allow belief in it to take hold in its followers. They feared that individuals would postpone and procrastinate their spiritual works under the premise of another chance in another lifetime. This is absurd, ofcourse, because one well-versed in reincarnation philosophy knows that any narrowing of consciousness and limitations in one lifetime must be discharged through an experience of equivalent action in a future lifetime. Who would want to enter a new life with such a predisposition? Do not jump to conclusions, however, that poor life circumstances are debts for bad karma in a previous lifetime. A spirit may have intentionally chosen painful circumstances in a lifetime in order to accelerate his spiritual development. It is critical then that we do not judge another's life circumstances.

As you can see in nature nothing is lost. The energy complex is carried to a future life until you penetrate the darkness of your consciousness and rise to the highest level of your Pure Self. The motivating force of Spirit is to meet in every experience that which will draw your spirit closer to Itself. Other people merely provide you the conditions to learn your lesson, make your path straight and in keeping with the Source, and to gain self-mastery. In relationships we merely meet ourselves through the law of nature which has no timetable.

Reincarnation is not a random system. You choose your next lifetime based on the lessons needed to be learned. Therefore, you are not a biological accident. You choose your parents. So let your parents off the hook for any dysfunction you may have experienced growing up. Rather ask yourself, "Why did I choose these parents and this family for my lifetime? What is it that I need to learn from this environment and its dynamics which I have chosen?" You might also want to ask yourself why you may have chosen a particular disease or financial limitations. It is because the process of going through these obstacles is the gift you yourself have chosen to test the metal of your soul's ability for your personal evolution. The greater insights one gains from these choices will help move one up the evolutionary ladder of the multidimensional consciousness.

According to quantum physics, however, something cannot "be there" until you can conceive it. You need, therefore, to conceive of your higher self as it is oscillating on the spectrum of the fourth dimension. Each step you take in applying and using this understanding will develop your ability to access past lives. Gain strength through knowledge of the fundamental principles of quantum energy. Then you can begin to add certain objective aspects of such experiences to yourself.

How would we explain homosexuality and transgender issues through reincarnation heredity, for instance, because neither psychology nor medicine, which emphasize overwhelmingly a third dimensional model of healing and are painfully limited to postnatal biography, can explain this growing phenomenon in our world today.

Psychoanalysis defines them as gender dysphoria. In most of these cases, psychoanalytic treatment is unsuccessful and at best brings about an adjustment to a lifestyle which does not feel inherently natural.

A female may feel "trapped" in a male body or vice versa. For many it is a life-threatening situation as they feel helpless to escape this cage-of-life especially for a transsexual. Suicide is frequently entertained. Other times, it leads to homosexual tendencies in adult life. For many the solution is electrolysis, analysis and hormonal therapy with an endocrinologist to prepare one for cross-living. After a year of cross-living, the transsexual person is evaluated for sex reassignment surgery which is typically a series of fifteen or more major surgeries over a period of several years in an attempt to change the sexual composition of an individual. In this way it is believed an individual can be made whole.

Rebirth philosophy, on the other hand, which sees us as multidimensional beings and transcends the third dimension, asserts another position for pulling oneself from darkness into light. It informs that more likely such individuals had a series of lives, but not necessarily all lives, lived in one gender. When too much maleness or femininity exists in an individual's psyche, a changeover is chosen by the person before the next incarnation to establish balance in conjunction with the concept of polarity. This causes gender-identity confusion and an uncertainty as to what gender one belongs because of the newness of the situation. Treatment might consist, therefore, of helping such individuals to access the lifetimes when this changeover took place to provide clarity and perspective on the present life time experience. Such individuals will see that in previous incarnations they were members of the opposite gender and in this lifetime were still clinging tenaciously to that role. As long as individuals keep focusing on a third dimensional model of life, they will never find permanent healing in any aspect of life.

Going through all these challenges which you choose from the spirit side will help you develop significant inner strength. They become transformational points for higher levels of consciousness and complexity for your soul's growth. You must become objective and impersonal to develop your ability in this spiritual science of life. Your higher consciousness from which all lifetimes evolve has a perennial wisdom not explainable by atomic sensory means. In all this work, the subtle and chakra/nadi systems never stop influencing and inputting into your physical vehicle.

Life is permanent at the causal spiritual levels and this is the chamber where all previous lifetimes are stored. At the physical level life is transitory. You can see how everything evolves out of a dynamic cycle. The cyclic interplay of these interdimensional forces of energy is a substantial component of quantum spirituality. It requires an understanding on your part of your invisible nature and your latent abilities. I would think by now you are already beginning to see that what you perceive is very different than your true nature and reality. Yet quantum physics informs us that you must conceive it to see it.

Your primary existence is at the timeless spaceless plane. As you continue to understand your invisible nature, you will then begin to notice how the threads of all forces, events and consciousness are woven into an unparalleled net of infinite relations. The distinction between the outer world and the inner world breaks down completely. They become fused into a unified undifferentiated whole. Your two worlds will meet. Your individuality will dissolve into the Oneness because there is no meaning to life as an isolated entity. If a path does not reveal your soul, it is of no use.

Life is full of mysteries. You need to be open-minded if you are going to understand the smallest fraction of this mystery. Without receptivity, you cannot hear the teacher of your inner voice. Progressive growth through receptivity will not happen all at once, but through deliberate effort and learning. In these efforts you will make errors. Errors are essential to improvement. Something is only a mistake if you don't learn from it; if you learn from it, it becomes a positive experience. Every experience challenges you to call on the best that is within you. The course and tenor of your quantum spirituality is determined by how well you listen to your inner voice. The heaps of convention and habits out of which society has made you, drown out your inner voice of growth by creating fixed mental patterns and a collective hypnosis which you now call reality. Be without conditioning because this mental norm is dramatically constricted. The answers are within you. Stop being someone you thought you were and start being your True Self.

Step into the spiritual dance of life with infinite opportunities and not just one brief cycle on the cosmic clock. Furthermore, if these incarnations provide you the opportunity to evolve from human (third dimension) to spiritual consciousness (fourth dimension), then you most probably have inhabited many life forms from mineral (first dimension) to animal (second dimension). Why would it be otherwise. The evolutionary cycle expands through a vast span.

Interdimensional studies through quantum spirituality provide you the psychic fuel to become a spiritual athlete and explore the minefield of your mind in a boundless process of existence. You will become the curator of your spirit and experience rapid spiritual development. The natural principles of the quantum spiritual life will fill you with vitality and aid you in exercising your spiritual muscles so they do not atrophy. The fact that you are reading this book is helping you stretch gently in preparation for your dance. Every page you read will expand your range of motion. It takes time to get in shape. Don't push the river.

Quantum spirituality with its interdimensional concepts is the work of living ideas; ideas that release the abilities and powers of your Spiritual Self rather than combining your consciousness into material form and pointing to its extinction with the decomposition of the physical form. You are an interdimensional being, a synthesis of energy fields of many different frequencies. Recognizing this is the way toward awakening your mind which has been imprisoned by unresolved chaotic energy through orthodoxy and conventions. Your suffering can be ended! You are a regenerative evolutionary spirit. Your atomic structure of your physical body is the smallest component of this Infinite Force. You will develop a further sense of freedom through this acceptance.

The Quantum Life moves you toward wholeness because it is the study of your immortal consciousness through the interrelation of all interdimensional phenomena. It is the study of the Infinite Plan. Quantum spirituality will help you with this acceptance because it will help you to differentiate between your physical third-dimensional self and your psychic-spiritual fifth-dimensional Self. The physical self is merely a vehicle for your spiritual self. It transports your spirit and sheds its atomic body at the end of each sojourn of third-dimensional life. When the physical self errs, however, the spiritual Self makes no judgment. Self knows these difficulties are a part of its soul's growth. This objectivity on your part is essential for full acceptance and full responsibility.

Life is a string of pearls. The pearls are your lifetimes and the Self is the thread. Once you have gained the recognition of yourself as an interdimensional being and accept full responsibility for your choices and behavior without expecting some external source to come rescue you, you will provide yourself with the freedom to grow by expanding your awareness and gaining a greater perception of reality. With this knowledge your soul will unfold, and you will develop rapidly your spiritual consciousness. You will awaken your innermost wisdom which is the Source of your higher inspiration. You will stop looking outward. You will experience a transcendence that is revolutionary and changes will occur in your life. You will not want to return to your previous sterile limits of ordinary physical consciousness!

The Quantum Life cuts through the limits of time and space and assists you in seeing yourself within the full framework of your Infinite Intelligence. When you dance with the Infinite, you dance with Yourself. From your present perspective this seems extraordinary. However, once your perspective becomes broadened, it will be quite natural. Every positive act in the direction of Source helps the light bulb shine brighter until it is all Light. Every negative act dims the light until it burns out and results in darkness. Self-knowledge of your interdimensional nature, however, requires patience, persistence and deliberate effort and one hundred percent responsibility.

THE MATERIAL WORLD IS
BOUND TO FAIL YOU

A person should so live that their happiness shall depend
as little as possible on external things
Epictetus

The outer trappings of your life are insignificant. For what are you searching in all your frantic activities that put you in a state of inconscience where there is no light? Become intoxicated with Spirit not with alcohol. Take one more inner trip, not one more outer trip. Renovate His house, do not buy a larger house. These are mere compensatory activities which leave you feeling apathetic. You are spinning out of control with all your activity. Your nervous restlessness and fitful use of materialism and alcohol consumption is your soul's indicator that it is still craving a connection with that which is not transient.

You are over filling your cup by being around others constantly. Your frequent social gatherings, often with the same people, are most likely filled with alcohol and intoxicants for escape, and will switch you off if only temporarily; poor music and mindless chatter which leave you more unfulfilled because nothing of depth has taken place due to having checked your prefrontal cortex at the door with your first alcoholic beverage. Alcohol and drugs distort the mind making it impossible to have any clarity. You will have no insight of any measurable value as long as alcohol and drugs are in your life. Furthermore, alcohol is pure sugar and sugar is a cancer magnet making it one of the reasons we have such a high rate of cancer in our nation. Today's non-artistic low-quality music should be of concern to you and to parents. Today's empty music is about money and stardom not about art. All this useless noise does not allow you to listen with your spirit. Although meaningful relationships, community, and friendships are very important in our lives, "empty" gatherings begin to lose their vitality and become your dope because you have become addicted to numbing your senses through them. When you must be with people all the time in idle chatter, these relationships become stagnant. These times for "chilling" then fill you with toxic energy rather than nourish you. You are numbed and neurotic by these gatherings because they create a painful division between your higher and lower self. More often than not, you are consuming energy that is unhealthy for your central nervous system. It leaves you feeling lonely and more isolated.

You know none of this is giving you solace because you are creating an inane vacuum with purely artificial meanings. Have you noticed at times how the emptiness of this reality leaves you exhausted after being in certain social gatherings? Instead of feeling recharged, you can barely wake up the next morning. You sleep in because you have depleted your energy rather than restored your energy. You are so trapped by your constant attraction to perpetual motion either through physical movement or useless chatter, that you continue to seek out this habitual temperament lest you become bored or depressed. This charade of standing above the crowd and endless futility is exhausting and unfulfilling. You have psychologically indoctrinated yourself influenced by orthodoxy. Examine it and downregulate the frenetic activity or you will continue to suffer endlessly. Unruly mind, unruly body. By continuing this lifestyle, all you are doing is postponing your ultimate frustration. You are frightened of sitting still aren't you because your intimacy with your soul is thin and vague. You are afraid to sit still because you do not want to feel the unexplained deep void in your heart. Your life has become an unproductive drudgery without your material dope by which you numb yourself. Living life large is a superficial philosophy when it places your soul in a state of acute crisis. Let your life instead be possessed by the mysterious reality of the active side of infinite consciousness. There is a greater purpose in life beyond your day-to-day frenetic activities.

You are a victim of an ignorant world that makes such feverish activity attractive. It is not the outside world that needs to change, however, it is the concept of yourself that needs to change that keeps you chasing your dope. This chase will consume you like a wildfire. You are about to drive yourself off a cliff unless you wake up in time to the fact that true joy only comes from within. If your cup is already full with all this feverish activity, there is no opportunity to fill it with something of greater substance and long-lasting value. Examine the times. Examine your life. Examine your distractions. Examine your boredom. Listen in silence to your boredom. It has something to teach you. Empty your cup and sit back objectively for a while. Sit in quietude. Do self-inquiry and witness objectively all that is going on around you.

Peace will never be attained in this way. You are in enemy territory. Beware. When all this self-centered activity stops, you will begin to touch silence and only then will you be capable of your fullest growth. Why are you so uncomfortable being silent? Why are you so uncomfortable being silent in the presence of another? Turn within, and still stay in touch with your environment. Just don't let yourself be pulled by your environment. Observe, don't absorb.

What are you teaching your children by your choices and behaviors? When our children in various life circumstances least know what to do, they fall back on what's most common. What is most common is what they saw happening in their family-of-origin. What are you teaching even adult children who are no longer living in your home? In what are they observing you participate which makes them think that what you have is what they need to live a happy life. Our children very naturally fall into resonance with our ideals. Are your ideals inspiring their hearts so they can fulfill *their* ideals? Reach inside so that you can let your consciousness reach right inside the consciousness of your children.

There is no limit to the darkness you can model for your children through self-indulgence. There is no limit to the Light you can model for your children by looking within. If you teach them to live from their soul, One Source will become everything for them as they access their unlimited capacity. In essence what they will be doing is uncovering all that they have already known. You choose. Perhaps you might want to let them watch you fill your cup drop-by-drop from the Ocean of Consciousness rather than drop-by-drop with that martini and useless chatter. Your soul sends you many divine inspirations. Perhaps you might want to listen to those inspirations. The way things look is deceptive. The only way to know the Truth is to go inward.

You are searching for your soul in all the wrong places by giving in to the pressurized reactionary elements of your life. Accumulate graces not more gold. I have never seen a Brinks truck follow a hearse yet. The less attachment, the more inner growth. If you look for substance in material things you will certainly be missing the mark because it is inner growth that matters. Boredom is your teacher. If you are still doing today what you were doing twenty or thirty years ago, pursuing excessive stimulation, there is something very neurotic in your personality on which you need to focus. Due to fears of insufficiency you shift and run from place to place and have lost your anchor. It is because most of our lives are out of balance that the Eastern medical system, Ayurveda, which is a 5000-year-old ancient medical model which comes to us from India, focuses on lifestyle for healing. It knows that you are so often over-heated from so much activity and motion that it keeps you fiery, anxious and out-of-balance because you are constantly activating and overstimulating the sympathetic nervous system.

Educate your feelings. This is the starting point to your spirituality. One of the most popular biblical verses reminds you to "Be still and know that I AM God." In your stillness, not frenetic activity, which keeps you addicted to constant external stimulation, you will learn about your I Amness, your original true nature. Only in simplicity will you rehabilitate yourself from this poverty of self.

I do not mean to deny nor diminish the importance of your earthly experiences for your spiritual growth. I am not suggesting that you take no interest in the external world or that you vacate into a Himalayan cave because escapism is not the answer. Nor do I suggest a life of indifference but one of discrimination because in the finite you can find the Infinite. It all depends on your approach and inner motivation. Do not give up your physical life, give up its illusions, so you can make your physical life a part of your spiritual life. Do not be enslaved by the material world.

You travel the world and you do not know yourself. Most people are on a trip without a goal. As your life is focused outward, make sure your eyes are focused inward. Transcend the material world while living in it. Let every outward action have inner significance. One small outward step may create a quantum inner leap. Every moment of life can be either a lesson or a school for learning. Look within! Life is a continuous education. Live in this world to be of service to others. Being in service to others gives meaning to your life and makes it a means for your self-realization. You will leave all material things behind, money, house, etc., and most of your time is spent on these external issues with very little time given to consciousness which is the goal of our existence. Your body also will one day fall victim to the worms, but your soul will continue to live. Speak less so the heart will lead. Few conversations are particularly brilliant. Teach through silence. Thirst more for the inner world. Look within!

La Rochefouchauld, a French writer commented, "When we are unable to find tranquility within ourselves, it is useless to seek it elsewhere." Be filled with reverence for the material world, but do not lose sight of your spiritual heritage. However, when you feel the material world has failed you, then look with your unbounded vision toward the Infinite because your essence is that of Source. You and Source are One. It is important to live life fully and yet rise above these lower limitations by looking from above.

Cherish what calls out to you whether it is valued by culture because orthodox culture is a pale shadow of a deeper order. Honoring your inner experience gives you a reliable map for the journey of your soul. The course and tenor of your spiritual life is determined by how well you listen to your inner voice. Yet this inner voice has its polarity, the dark side, which is in constant dialectical process with your higher consciousness. This intra-polarity is the best and worst that is found in a person. In order to develop integration and transformation, you need to cancel out as much of what is contained in the negative polarity. The lessons learned from the struggles of the negative polarity within you will result in wholeness. Do not suppress them. Rather make them conscious and understand them. Be a creative work of art in the constant and continuous process of remaking yourself while in the service of Infinite Intelligence. This beauty carries with it an incomprehensible power! You will never forget a person with such an exceptional and striking phenomenon.

Annihilate any ego until your divine love grows into perfection. Metamorphose your perceptions of material allures until you are nothing but the Divine and until you are filled with God-consciousness! Go inward as you will only find Spirit in silence.

The whole world is asleep in the arrogant conditioning and narrow outlook of culture and generation. Stop bowing down to protocol as if in a court. Develop an independence of thought and an exuberance of spiritual energy so friends will never forget you and they will carve you infinitely into their memories. Do not be flooded and hypnotized by wrong doctrines and dogmas. Broadcast instead only Truth and divine living. Seek refuge only in Source not in a church. Why would you, One Source, go to a building with four walls looking for yourself? It is yourself that you are seeking. You must be firm as a rock in your convictions and sincerity and live with an inexplicable joy so you can walk yourself Home wide awake. Do you dare wake up and let your embryonic consciousness evolute from Homo Sapiens to Homo Spiritualis?

THERE IS NO BEGINNING, THERE IS NO END

You are Divinity. So is a grain of sand. God is the substratum of your being. God is the substratum of being in the grain of sand. This is the beginning. When you were born, you were pure spirit inspired into form. Yet you are a split second on the cosmic clock.

Our good fortune is that there is no monopoly on God. He is the common property of all of us and in everything. The same Infinite Ocean forms the waves. Just like ice changes form when it melts into water, so does God change His form to transition into man. God is the Universal Soul and you are Its emanation. Only that which is born will die. Your physical body only is born. Your physical body is time bound and temporary. Your Spirit is unborn and deathless and does not change with time. Therefore, you are Spirit, deathless and infinite. God is Infinite; therefore, so must you be.

Infinity has no beginning and no end. If there was a beginning then God would not be Infinite. You have no beginning and no end. You have always existed and you will not die. Life does not stop when the heartbeat flatlines. Death, which in Latin means change, is a mirage! Death at the end of a life cycle is a myth because the continuity of life is a basic mandate of the construct of energy. Has anyone told you that? Death is an exhale that will not be followed by an inhale. Death is merely the body changing the garment that you wear. You are eternal. You have, rather, been conditioned to believe in perishability. You have been taught that consciousness arises from your physical body, and, consequently, vanishes with its dissolution. If you want to continue squandering your life in a limited belief that you are nothing more than a sensory body, then your belief in perishability is a natural conclusion and you will continue to move into a soulic apocalyptic and eschatological disaster. The Quantum Life elucidates that energy can only be regenerated and transformed,

61

it cannot be destroyed. Quantum spirituality is rooted in living ideas. Living ideas are ideas of infinity, immortality and imperishability which empower. Living ideas release you rather than confine your consciousness in physical form.

At death a cycle is concluded but your life is not concluded. Death cannot take anything from you because birth gave you nothing. Death as an end to life is another myth you have been conditioned to believe. Your body is merely a visitor; it will come and it will go; treat it as such with the greatest of reverence because it is the temple of your Spirit. Death is an interval between your incarnations and an entrance into a fuller life. In death you merely withdraw your consciousness from the third dimension and become actively conscious on the fourth dimension. You have done it many times already. However, if you are still worried, then buy yourself some "death insurance" by tithing to your priest, rabbi or minister who will promise you that your afterlife is cared for!

At the end of any cycle you merely shed your shell like the caterpillar when it metamorphoses into the butterfly. "What the spirit calls the end of life, the Master calls the butterfly," instructed Richard Bach. You will have a sense of having been asleep and just awakened. You will continue your life in the spirit world within a few moments, hours, or days in an astral environment, an environment which will be compatible with your evolutionary state. Death is an awakening, while birth is a death for the spiritual world. Death is the ascension of your spirit. Death is the stream of change in the interdimensional cycle of your life. It is a graduation into a freer and happier dimension and a central aspect to self-renewal. Begin today walking yourself Home with grace, dignity and awareness. Earth is not your Home. Yet rest assured that when you leave, the entire energy field is influenced.

The end of an earth cycle is a most marvelous wondrous moment in the experience of life's grand design. A moment of closer vision and proximity with Infinite Intelligence. It is beyond this point that you get the full vision of Infinite Creative Intelligence. Learn courageously to embrace death. Therefore, an attitude of calm positiveness and serene acceptance toward a cycle's end is critical in order to release yourself from the emotional fear of death. Master the art of dying through daily meditation so you do not attempt to cling to life as long as possible under the influence of narcotics which will trap your inert body. The solution to the opioid crisis is now available and it is simple, but it does not favor big pharma! Opioids interfere with the mind's ability to give form to potentia. Narcotics frustrate your transition by creating a conflict in you when consciousness is attempting to relinquish its tenacious hold on its physical existence.

Meditation will aid in maintaining a soulic effort into the hour of death because we must cast a finer net to not let consciousness slip through. The rise and fall of the breath in meditation is a constant reminder of the ebb and flow process of each moment of conscious life. A consciousness free from limitations and conditioning at time of death will aid you in the transition in the afterlife and will aid your spirit into a higher rebirth state.

You did not originate here. You will be going back Home. You will be coming back again and again, however, until you perfect love by acknowledging and knowing Self. Make love the lord of your life and you will become fearless. Love for the Whole. Create a love revolution because heartfelt love transforms. Love opens your heart for Spirit to enter. You will continue to come back to planet earth until you perfect love and until you know that Consciousness is the ground of being; there is nothing but Consciousness.

Death is a process of self-renewal. Death is when you will become One with the Infinite Source. It is an ascension of your spirit from the captivity of your physical form. You change from an atomic body to an energy system of Light. Therefore, death is merely a change in frequency. Soulic spirit energy oscillates at millions and millions of megahertz per second in comparison to human thought which oscillates only at hundreds of megahertz per second contrasted with home electrical energy which oscillates at sixty cycles per second.

Birth and death, this back-and-forth movement, are the alpha and omega, of the spiritual dance of life. So critical to constantly listen to your inner voice so you can evolute to your highest potential in each cycle. There will come a time when you will no longer need to incarnate on earth for your own personal learned experiences because your earthly education will be completed. However, you might choose to incarnate to teach, to lead and to inspire in order to help others grow spiritually. So be aware, that we touch one another's lives for a reason. Everyone is our teacher. Everyone is ourselves. Nothing in life happens by accident. No one crosses your path without a reason.

Some know the moment that they will leave their mortal coils. It is possible to be in good health and choose the time and day of your death as a conscious exit from your body, mahasamadhi. Paramahansa Yogananda, an advanced spiritual master from the East, was sent to America by his guru to spiritualize America. In the 1950s, he was speaking to a large crowd and informed them that at the end of his talk he will make his transition. He dropped to the floor and left his body. His body did not decompose.

My beloved mother also made a conscious exit from her physical body. I brought my mother to live with us at ninety years of age so she could finish well. One evening she and I were in the sitting room and per our usual discussions I was very interested in historical insights directly from her especially related experiences of World War II since she lived through them and I am a post war baby. I was kneeling by her legs near her wheelchair, as not to miss a word she said since she always spoke softly, and unexpectedly she whispered to me, "I am not going to enjoy you any longer." I inquired, "What do you mean mother?" "I am not going to enjoy you any longer," she repeated with a slight soft smile on her face. I asked, "Do you mean you are going to Jesus?" knowing that she had a strong Catholic faith. She smiled and nodded her head, "Yes." I put my head on her lap and wept profusely. That night I tucked her in, went through our evening ritual of kissing her forehead, kissing her nose, then her lips and singing a short lullaby as my tears washed her face and concluded by articulating my infinite love for her.

The next morning I sat at the edge of her bed, filled with anticipatory grief, trepidation and devastation that she might truly not awaken. Then she opened her eyes. She smiled largely. She chuckled. We both understood. I smiled. No words were necessary. No explanations needed. My mother knew I was not ready for her transition. She waited for me to master my internal resistance. For the next two weeks, she prepared me for her transition through the images of the night. I dreamt her transition daily. Dreams are a continuation of the polarized movement of our consciousness. My mother would show herself in these nocturnal scenarios with my two older brothers who had both preceded her into the Spirit world. These dreams were highly personal and a part of my soul's growth. These dreams were my guide with the potential to help me break out of a groove in which I was; a groove of attachment, of not wanting to let go. These "visions" affected me to the very depths of my being and were predictive. At the end of those two weeks, my beloved mother shed her physical body.

I was with her during the moment of her transition. She "died" in my arms. She began to breathe faster and faster and I could hear the Cheyne-Stokes breathing and then the death rattle. These were signs that her body was beginning to shut down. I watched her skin color change from very purple to pure white. In an attempt to assist her transition, I softly whispered, "Evan, Evan, Evan, you have labored very hard for ninety-two years, take your last breath!" She drew her last breath. With that final vital breath, my mother dropped her physical body and her "I Amness" went to the Absolute. With that final exhalation she opened the doors to eternity joining hands with the bliss of the Supreme. I placed my head on her bosom, embracing her body and covering it with my tears.

Death, a point of expression in life and a normal sequence in our evolutionary cycle, is like changing your pillow case; the pillow is not destroyed in this change. You cannot keep the same pillow case on forever. It wears out. It cannot provide you infinite use any more than your body can provide infinite use. So you shed it. Some learn the many ways of leaving the body and others just await the moment. Death is a more perfect life because you oscillate at a higher frequency and being recharged by a greater positive field. This is the cosmic movement of life. You are a constantly moving river with an active mind functioning interdimensionally.

Your heart craves the Infinite. Your heart throbs to its infinite capacity. You will find Infinite Intelligence in the deep recesses of your human heart. Persist until you get a glimpse of the Unknown. Continue to make valiant attempts until you know the Oneness with the Infinite. The illusion of differences between the Infinite and the finite must melt away under the scorching rays of your devotion. Beg and plead to never "miss the mark" because the separation from the Divine is worse than being in a dungeon. Do not let your heart get lacerated; rather, purify it with thoughts of Infinite Source. Beg to be His favored child to reach your Ultimate Goal and unite with your Father of Light. Become a formidable force in search of knowing this Infinite Intelligence because knowing Source is the noblest privilege you can receive rather than a source of degenerative indoctrinated fear as the "God" of orthodoxy. Becoming informed is done through spirituality not intellectuality. This is done through natural health not prescription or street drugs. This is done through your interior self not doctrines. This is done through silence not distractions. Investigate abstruse truths, ponder over them, then assimilate and absorb them. You will not find these truths in the market places of the world but through inner silence. Only in silence will you equip yourself for Perfection. Silence always embraces integration. This is our common goal.

God-consciousness is the ground of being; there is nothing but Consciousness. There is no real power outside of you! Create your own world by raising yourself from the dead fiction of your life. Direct your own destiny by thinking outside the box. It is the stretch of these conceptions that will light your way into Infinity. See the Light behind the shadow and set your soul on fire so that you may make your transition from planet earth to the Light world in the highest vibration of yourself. Pure truth and right action of your dynamic consciousness. There is a better way to live!

EXAMINING CRUCIAL QUESTIONS

I myself did not get here overnight. Self-awakening called me to action and it took many different paths and processes to reach my awakening. The search for understanding was often unsettling. I searched and explored many different meditations and traditions. It was an absorbing quest. Yet, we all need to give birth to a wisdom tradition entirely our own, especially since our culture suffers from a crisis of perception and shallow awareness. It may take a long time to overcome this crisis, but in the long run you will be rewarded with deep insights into the true nature of spirituality.

I had to examine crucial questions that no one could answer for me in order to discover the seeds of a spiritual life that works for me. "Am I only the body?" "If there is more, then what is there?" "What is this thing called consciousness?" "Am I just an outward flow of life or do I have an inner life?" "What do I really believe?" "Is there more to life than this?" "What beliefs are mine and what comes from my history and society?" "Is there death?" Don't be afraid of the vacuum all these questions will create. Have the courage to stay in the vacuum for a while. Be a witness to whatever arises. This silence becomes meditative. If you meditate over a question, it will allow for the answers to come through. This calm inner self will bring to you many answers. It becomes your bridge from the outer to the inner. These questions were the stirrings of my awakening as these thoughts shaped my life.

The biggest spiritual challenge in this self-inquiry was how much of my environment do I create? What responsibility do I shoulder in all that goes on in my world? I concluded that I create all of it. I asserted that my assumptions, conscious or unconscious, about anything or anyone influenced people's behaviors in my life, bear fruit in my reality, and shaped my life and relationships. These assumptions build a bridge of incidents that lead me to the end result. I concluded that others merely are bearing witness to that which I thought about them and played out for me the conversations I may have in my head about them. I began experimenting changing those conversations and those people or circumstances miraculously changed! Life circumstances are always playing out for us the movies in our minds. Run your own experiment and see your results. Because I no longer wanted to live in a fictitious world, I ran a significant number of experiments of my own before I felt convinced. Change your assumptions, and you will change your reality because all of creation exists within you.

I offer in The Quantum Life my personal touchstones which have aided me in my spiritual development and which have served as "step-ups" in my consciousness. Various activities have allowed me to discover and activate my own creative birthright. I no longer am willing to accept the world in the way that it presents itself to me without. I assert my supremacy. I take control from the inside out.

My own personal spiritual journey was no overnight affair. It has taken me from Catholicism to Christianity, to Judaism, to Buddhism and other spiritual philosophies. I journeyed through the exploration of Christian mystics such as Jesus, a mystical yet political figure with great magnitude of importance to the entire human race. Yet, the face of Jesus that is known belonged to the history of a particular time. I journeyed through the life of medieval Italy's St. Francis of Assisi, a true Christian visionary and a champion of the poor whose divine rapport with animals and the natural world radiated joy in every cell within me. Francis-fever is contagious. If you have not yet viewed the movie "Brother Son, Sister Moon," the life story of St. Francis of Assisi, you may want to consider doing so.

I inhaled the works of contemplatives such as Thomas Keating, our beloved Dutch priest; Henri J. M. Nouwen, who died unexpectedly in 1996; and the inspiring works of Thomas Merton, a Trappist monk and seminal figure in dialogue on Christianity–Buddhism who died in Thailand in 1968 electrocuted by a defective fan in his lodgings. I read the Christian Bible, both the old and new testament, every Lenten season for ten years. Since I had often felt more Jewish than I did Roman, I began attending Jewish Temples, studied and practiced various Jewish spiritual practices, explored the history of the bigness and greatness of the Jews whose history is of tremendous significance in all our lives, chanted in front of a bronze Hanukkah Menorah, celebrated Rosh Hashanah, and listened to the Torah. I have been inspired by the treasured writings of Kahlil Gibran and challenged by the works of Alan Watts who bridged the east and west in an unprecedented manner.

Remembering that Jesus had significant eastern influence, I began journeying to India, read and re-read the accumulated treasury of spiritual laws in the Bhagavad Gita. I prostrated myself at their temples. I studied the spiritual works of Asia's most highly acclaimed gurus such as Paramahansa Yogananda's self-realization three-year course which initiated me in Kriya Yoga. I contemplated the works of the venerable Dalai Lama who gifted me with his autobiography and a personally blessed mala when I visited in his home in the Himalayas where he is exiled, and read the works of Thich Nhat Hanh, our beloved Vietnamese monk.

My own search reminds me of the bamboo of Eastern Asia. The seed for the bamboo is planted, and for five years the members of a community water this seed every day taking turns. Yet day after day after day for five years, no sprout is visible. Then suddenly, the bamboo sprouts and rapidly grows to eighty-feet high!

I encourage you to look more deeply at life and allow the time for the seed of your spirituality to be watered from within you. Your spirituality is the most important journey of your life. Your spirituality is a very personal relationship with your God. The most violent act I know is for one to impose his spiritual views on another human being. This is soul violence! I hope my personal journey may be a means of activating a lever, particularly in this new cycle, to open your perception to a wholesome spiritual reality and keep you intoxicated with Spirit. Which brings to memory another period in my life.

I remember the village "idiot" when I lived in Europe for the first eleven years of my life. He would come out mostly in the evenings, sometimes naked, sometimes clothed, playing hide and go seek throughout the neighborhood, swaying, dancing and laughing. His laughter rang out strongly like a bell; whereas, at other times, he would be utterly silent. He seemed to use dance as a tool to awaken his energy. He danced in the streets, threw his hands up to the sky to salute the heavens, then opened them widely in a gesture of receptivity to the abundance of the universe. A "sun salutation" perhaps without his needing to know what that meant. He prayed and sang with his body. His mind failed him they would say. Whose mind failed whom I often wonder.

I marvel on how he lived intimately with the powerful forces of his inner world, totally uninhibited and fully expressive clothe only in the cosmos. He ran around in mindless skipping, hiding and screaming and laughing. His sounds would echo throughout the village. He abandoned himself ecstatically into dance awaiting his audience. Like the Pied Piper or St. Francis, wherever he went there would be a flock of giggling little creatures around him. We followed him into the fields skipping and laughing, as adults watched through their windows and locked their doors and hearts more tightly. The nightly crowd of children followed him around and imitated his dance and gestures. His movements seemed transcendental in experience.

Was he foolish or insane or was he "bliss-intoxicated?" Was he utterly crazy as perceived by western traditions, or was he a spiritually emerging, unpredictable and God-absorbed Indian *avadbuta* as known by the Hindus? Furthermore, the *sannyasin* saints of Jainism, an offshoot of Hinduism, went about "clothed in space," stark naked to totally eliminate any social pretensions.

In our Western culture, we often make negligible distinction between mysticism and psychopathology. The Okinawan culture would call the village "idiot" a *kamidori*, or alchemist meister. Mystical experiences are often in great contradiction to all common sense and to classical Western world view. The Muslim Sufi's would perceive him as a Divinely enraptured *majdhub*. We indiscriminately dismiss and ignore the contribution made by the great spiritual traditions in our understanding of the psyche and human nature. The Buddhists would embrace him as a *yu-jen,* a leader, totally freed from his ego, the Hasidics as a *tzaddikim.* Nevertheless, it is useful to accept that some behaviors are sad, but not necessarily mad; while others are sad, mad, and bad.

Who really is insane? Who really is the idiot? The "idiot" tried to bring us out under the sky and the breeze and the moon. Night after night he danced through the village, and night after night, only the children would follow. The adults could only receive his dance through a window. The children needed no windows. They only needed the sky. Jesus said, "Until you become like children, you will not enter the kingdom of heaven." It is as if the village "idiot" deliberately hid by day from the tasteless pleasures of the world, and emerged by night to experience the light of true Self without distraction. He was delightfully uninhibited. He had not been mind-controlled and conditioned like the rest of the population. He danced to the beat of his own drum and there are few of us strong enough to do it today. The "idiot's" story reminds me of the Zen koan of the frog in the well who believed the well to be the greatest ocean until he saw the real ocean. Might we still be in the well, and the "idiot" in the ocean?

In another situation I recall struggling with an issue the content of which I no longer remember. What I do remember is that I had an intellectual vision of a voice that identified itself as Archangel Gabriel. I chuckled and dismissed it after I laughingly demanded, "If you are truly Archangel Gabriel speaking to me, then give me a sign!" That afternoon my husband and I needed to go to a nearby town about 1-1/2 hours away. He was driving, I was the passenger, so I had plenty of time to enjoy the beautiful forested scenery. I knew the terrain and signs on this rural road like the back of my hand because it was a drive I made every week for ten years to get to my clinical office. Three-quarters of the way into our drive, was a huge sign to the right of the road that said: Archangel Gabriel Church (new construction)!

Synchronicities are a crosswalk between mind and matter, not connected by direct cause and effect, but by quantum effects. This was a homing beacon that I was on the right path with the message coming to me from an administrator of the Plan. I do not ignore these intuitive hits. I examine them like a crucial question and embrace them. These intuitive hits are winks and nods from the universe. These synchronicities are orchestrated by Source, another way It speaks to us. In this higher area of intuition, the concept may not always be clear, but I attune to these synchronicities. More anima as Carl Jung would say, more opportunities for listening to our inner Self. Our spiritual journey is an eternal journey of constantly examining crucial questions and experiences through different streams of consciousness that is constantly flowing. Think big! It is all a movement of Source and the greatest adventure!

CONSCIOUSNESS IS NOTHINGNESS

The foundation of Quantum Spirituality is Consciousness. Without Consciousness there would be no spark in our lives nor would we have a life. We would be barren like a desert. Consciousness is awareness. It is the original basic existence and the Source of everything. It is the doorway into the Light. Yet Consciousness is hard to define because it is in constant unfoldment. It is the vehicle through which Intelligence expresses Itself. You are a physical expression of this Intelligence clothe in an organic gown of flesh, changing form made from Infinite stardust.

Consciousness is an infinity of vibrations that eventually produces grosser vibrations that collapse into matter. Everything in our third dimensional world emanates from Consciousness through electromagnetic frequency. You are an emanation of Consciousness which underlies the foundational nature of all that exists. Everything is a mighty pulsation of Consciousness which is Nothingness. Therefore, everything visible is empty. The gestalt of matter is all underwritten by Consciousness which is homogenous, but it does have heterogenous embodiments. You and I are those embodiments. The Self is all–one. The explicate order from the implicate order. There is unity in this diversity which comes from the Life Force that resides in every cell of our body. Protons and electrons join together to form our physical anatomy through downward causation which renders us equal in Divinity but not equal in consciousness because we are all at different evolutionary stages.

Everything Visible Is Empty

Consciousness is everywhere and cannot be affected by anything. You cannot take away from It. Therefore, you cannot "sin" against Consciousness. You depend on Consciousness to exist, but Consciousness does not depend on you for its existence. When you shed your mortal coils and no longer exist in the material form, Consciousness still exists because it has no material limitations. It is the multi-dimensional field of your body with matter being its shadow. It existed before matter, and matter is Consciousness collapsed. Access Consciousness for an inward revolution because becoming conscious is the sole purpose of our incarnation. "Do you have the courage to be who you really are?" questions Pir Vilayat Inayat Khan.

Defining Consciousness through language becomes relatively difficult and feels inadequate. It comprises a very subtle theme and dimension of information. Consciousness is nondualistic awareness that is all pervasive and infinite. It is active everywhere and it is all there is. Because it is infinite, it is impossible to completely define it because the minute you define it, the definition has already become irrelevant and outdated. Our entire third dimensional world emanates from Consciousness through electromagnetic frequency that exists below all physical matter. There is nothing in which you cannot find Consciousness. Yet, let us be clear here. You do not have Consciousness. Consciousness, formless, has assumed your form. You are a part of the whole: Microcosmos = Macrocosmos! Nothing = Everything!

Consciousness is unbounded, limitless, nonspatial, timeless and the Infinite Present. It is the modus operandi behind your life functions through electro-magnetic bio-information. Understanding Consciousness is the fundamental premise of your life because in you there is a coherent organizational process composed of diversified and interacting systems and levels: Consciousness, supramental, mental, vital and physical. I liken these levels to our academic system of elementary school, middle school, high school, undergraduate and graduate school. They all have a life of their own, but interconnected with varying degrees of vitality amongst them.

Consciousness is timeless, ageless, and endless. It never grows old. It has the same properties of the Infinite Creative Intelligence just like the wave in the ocean has the same properties as the rest of the water in the ocean. The only difference is in volume. It is spiritual, eternal, self-renewing and regenerative. It is the creative principle of the universe, and thought is its eternal energy. Express it in all its beauty and glory! In order to do that, however, you need to get beyond the narrow "normal" world of third-dimensional sensory perception. You need to understand the reality of Consciousness, a reality of a fourth and fifth dimensional nature, which gives meaning to the absurd patchiness of your sensory world. Your Higher Consciousness has a perennial wisdom not explainable by Newtonian physics and atomic sensory means. Quantum attributes of Consciousness do not follow Newtonian laws. The Quantum Life, however, discloses that spatio-temporal limitations of Self are merely optical illusions! You may think you are a physical body, but what you are is Consciousness. Go inward and you will get beyond the optical illusions. There is a better way to live!

Consciousness is never born and never dies! It is your Generator. Your body and your organs are mere habitual instruments. The nature of Consciousness is Infinity, Bliss and Self-awareness. It is all there is and everything is initiated as a function of Consciousness and it is behind all that exists. This is the quantum life.

Consciousness is a dynamic system, constantly changing and not a stable fixed thing. It is a complicated energy system, but there is no reason to believe that the energy which runs your consciousness is any different than the energy which runs the universe. As you increase the energy of your mind through meditation, you will experience greater individuation because there is no limit to the ability of your Consciousness other than those stemming from your own belief system. Orthodoxy definitely limits the development of physical consciousness because of the bondage it has put you in which barricades the Light and makes it run amuck. Your physical consciousness requires Light to see its way into Greater Consciousness which is always transcending and expanding.

You need to remove your negative unconscious beliefs that something cannot be done. Since you are hypnotized from infancy by orthodoxy, your prime task as an adult is to dehypnotize yourself. You need to know that your perceived world is illusory with another reality behind it. Much of what you think is true is a false collective belief made difficult to check because most of the rest of the world shares the same belief. Stop being a robot. There is a better way to live.

In quantum energy/medicine/spirituality all five levels of consciousness, supramental, mental, vital and physical must be considered to determine the etiology of a medical condition. The physical manifestation is a stepped-down version of the subtle disharmony. The quantum physician must determine at which of the subtle levels the imbalance originally happened before it manifested in the physical and treat that level. It takes a very experienced quantum practitioner to make these distinctions and treat accordingly.

The Quantum Life is not mere erudition of scholarly knowledge. Rather it takes you into what is unchanging in the changing phenomenon of the world. It directs you toward your Ultimate Self. It recognizes the unity behind the diversity in our physical environment. It teaches you how to live in the medium of Consciousness like fish live in the sea and birds in the air effortlessly. It instructs you in suzerainty over material possessions. The Quantum Life nudges you further to set the right value on what the world offers. It crosses the limits of the material world to conceive of Consciousness in the healing of your soul. Your sole responsibilities in your evolutionary process are conception and conviction. Let us do the Great Work together.

The Quantum Life informs you that you are not a mere physical body, but also an astral (subtle body) and causal body (Consciousness). These bodies interpenetrate one another and create a life sustaining energy that circulates throughout your various subtle bodies from the third to the fifth dimension. It is the causal body that enfolds the other bodies into itself. In the descriptive sense they are five bodies. In the dynamic sense, however, they are only One body since they are all fourth dimensional except for the physical. They are dynamic, non-dualistic and constantly changing.

You need to awaken to the fact that you are not locked within the tether of physical time, conventions, or physical body. Rather, you have everything you need for wholesome existence when you access Consciousness which is a perfect equilibrium of pure life force, spirituality and energy. Expect and accept. Consciousness is your parent atom, your Father of Light, your Source, your God. It contains every specific characteristic to produce itself and develop through the evolutionary cycle into the recognition of its infinite properties again from which it originally derived.

You are gestating Infinity with a mind that is in constant communication with unseen forces in higher dimensions and unknown worlds. Your higher dimensional Self picks up events before your third dimensional self has any awareness. This has been reflected in research that has shown enlarged pupils seconds before an incident occurs. Dare to live your quantum life in your fullness not your smallness. You have non-physical abilities way beyond your physical body.

This gestating infinity is the functionary process of your interconnected energies in all five of your bodies which result in a never-ending movement of Infinity within you. This is your existence to which you need to awaken in order to regain your identity with Infinite Creative Intelligence from where all your spiritual healing is possible. "Everything is energy. That's all there is to it," Albert Einstein. Do not let orthodoxy take away all that you are.

Be curious about life. Go beyond the ephemeral into the Infinite and look beyond your localized bundle of cells and organs and tissues and cartilages that make up your physical body. The Quantum Life helps you to open up your own wisdom library by teaching you to access deeper levels of Consciousness for your spiritual healing. It encourages you to wake up to who you truly are and allow your Infinite Self to unfold Itself. This in turn, accelerates your spiritual evolution by helping you to move from a knee-jerk skepticism, powerlessness, and the powerful opium of orthodox conditioning and conventions. It is a shift from external authority to inner knowing. Quantum life and quantum spirituality make it clear that there is something bigger and greater inside of you which remains untapped and can be accessed by a shift in Consciousness. There is a central phenomenology in this spiritual self-healing in which "absolute" knowledge is available in transpersonal fields and from which everything else arises! Draw on that Absolute knowledge in your self-unfolding.

The Quantum Life delineates with exceptional clarity your interdimensional nature and shifts this perennial mystery into a spiritual healing paradigm. This is a new vision and opportunity toward your spiritual evolution. You must tap Consciousness if you want to awaken from your mass hypnosis which has limited your freedom and suspended your waking self. You must tap Consciousness if you want to do your own thinking and end your innocence that has caused you to live an unfulfilling existence. It is up to you now. You no longer need to be a robot. Wake up. It is your prime task and only yours to dehypnotize yourself. You have such enormous potential and you are standing in your own way. There is a better way to live by tapping into your Collective Spirit through the quantum life. It links you with the regenerative intelligence of infinite evolution. You emerged from the Collective Spirit and you will merge back into the Collective Spirit.

When Rene Descartes, a creative mathematician of the first order, a scientific thinker and metaphysician, commented, "I think, therefore, I am," he was mistaken, and at that moment he originated the mind/body split with which you have been indoctrinated. This split is very much foundational to orthodox conditioning. This split, this duality, is one of the initial tales imposed on your development that separated you from your spirituality. You must "be" before you can think. Therefore, you existed in Consciousness before any thought, as thought is a product of Consciousness. The Quantum life holds a spirito-bio-philosophical view of mind/body and states that Consciousness, nondualistic awareness, collapses thought. Thought does not have the capacity to bring about nondualistic activity. You can increase this nondualistic awareness as much as you want because you are infinite. However, when you project your Consciousness outward it becomes filtered by the brain creating limitations at this point. You need to venture inward into your Silence and reverse the flow of energy for authentic resolutions. Even Jesus Christ clearly informed and directed you repeatedly, "The kingdom of God is within you." This inward focus is the single-mindedness in the process of your spiritual evolution through quantum living. Look within and feel your consciousness rising! "I am indestructible consciousness, protected in the bosom of Spirit's immortality," Paramahansa Yogananada.

You came from the Ocean of Immortality and you will return to the Ocean just like the Azure Window in the front cover photograph of this book which I captured during my last visit to Gozo, Malta in

Europe. I remember swimming and splashing my way back and forth cautiously to this iconic beauty in the Mediterranean Sea. The Azure Window, an organ of the consciousness of the Maltese Islands where I was born and raised, developed through sea erosion resulting from wave action. The continued activity resulted in upward formations of a joint which eventually became wider. First it formed a cave and then it formed an arch. The end of the life cycle of this icon believed to have existed for 500 years resulted on March 8, 2017, after a period of heavy storms. Initially, one of the pillars gave way, and then the arch collapsed right with it. The Azure Window came from the Ocean and it collapsed back into the Ocean. On March 8, 2017, the life cycle of this monumental limestone natural carving came to an end. We bid it farewell as we extend our gratitude for 500 years of immeasurable visual delight. Change is a constant and inevitable feature of all life.

We also were collapsed into our physical form from the Ocean, and we also shall collapse right back into the Ocean of Consciousness as we merge back into our Light bodies after a life cycle and fuse into the "bosom of Spirit's immortality." We, as the Azure Window, reflect the fusion of the infinite and the finite, the tenacity of our divine and human spirits, and the power and unpredictability of life with all its commensurate drama. In the quantum life, we are constantly breaking the bounds of what is possible. We live to the immutable laws of consciousness and nature. We cannot separate the two and to do so is implausible without showing pure lack of scholarship.

STOP COURTING SLAVERY

The Quantum Life emphasizes continuously the enormous powers that your conditioned beliefs have, and how your education and culture have stunted your spiritual development. Cultural conditioning has hindered your inner self by teaching you separations and boundaries that are illusory. Herd allegiance has cut you off from your higher self and inner wisdom by keeping you courting slavery because this cultural hypnosis has overthrown your human mind by making you believe that you are a finite limited being. You have been convinced that you are man or you are woman when you are God-Consciousness. You are Source. You cannot and never will lose the consciousness of this identity with Infinite Creative Intelligence. Why is it so easy to believe the former but not the latter? Renounce the false self. Unplug yourself from such rigid perceptions which you are holding. The Quantum life urges you to take charge of the "kingdom of God that is within you!" You are Absolute Reality and do not let anyone tell you any differently. Live from the Absolute biune of Oneness and individuation into your self-expression into the Infinite. You are Divine and you will return to the Divine. There is no other way.

The Quantum Life very clearly communicates that life is about learning and evolving and that multiple lives and rebirths facilitate that process. You will surely keep coming back again and again until you experience Infinite Intelligence within yourself. This grand design of life is the continuity of Consciousness from life to life, a god-like extravaganza that is positively biased and taps into the vastness of your infinite capabilities. It is a homeopathic move to go with what is inherent within you and look beyond the common "normal" view. The Quantum Life is a distillation of your spiritual evolution that aids in revealing your interior self. This makes all options available toward your spiritual development and healing. It helps you to uncover your native state of being, that of nothingness, which is infinite. Wake up. There is a better way to live.

You need to integrate and align the causal, subtle and physical so they are conflict free and directed toward the same end. You need to get beyond the narrow world of third-dimensional sensory perception which is the first order of reality. You need to grasp the second order of reality, a reality of a fourth-dimensional nature which gives meaning to the absurd patchiness of your sensory world. Your higher consciousness has a perennial wisdom not explainable by atomic sensory means. Spatio-temporal limitations of Self are merely optical Illusions!

Create a quantum entanglement with Source. This entanglement literally alters your enzymes and hemoglobin values. It has a biological effect as noted in blood samples via microscopy and EEGs. Your spiritual healing, however, can never happen from the physical/brain level but rather from the larger field when you align with Infinite Source. Once you cleanse your doors of perception, you will see that everything is Infinite Creative Intelligence. There is nothing but this Infinite Intelligence that is constantly regenerating. You are a never-ending succession of the regeneration of Consciousness. You will always keep tapping on a subtle interdimensional field of infinite information. In this infinite perspectus, you will never arrive at a point in evolution where you will see a cessation of this interplay of harmonic principle.

I am asserting that all existence is one Being. This Being is Consciousness. Consciousness is the infinite play of existence. Consciousness is your divine source which is imperishable. Consciousness is your real Self which you have forfeited and hidden underneath all the conditioning. Stop courting slavery. You have to unveil your real Self if you want to achieve your divinity.

The entire architecture of your Being is made up of the subtle and the physical. This is the entire panoply of your life in which different aspects of Consciousness are viewed from its component parts. This is the entire rendition of the score of the Master. The Master is illimitable but you were conditioned to believe in a limited individuality. Because of this limited understanding, you have limited everything; and, therefore, identified with all the wrong things. It is this limited understanding that causes you to believe you were born in sin. You are free of sin. You are never small. You only have been convinced that you are small. As you change your awareness you will change your world.

Consciousness is the Source that appears through the media of the gross and the subtle. There is no place where Consciousness is not. Your life is interdimensional in scope. Look within and find your strength. Once you close your eyes you will find the treasure of an incredible experience because you will have the awareness that you and Source are One rather than you and Source are different. As long as you continue to clutch on to that infantile belief that God is outside of you, you will never have peace. And if there is no peace within you, there will never be peace in our world. God is within you. You are the one who creates your own heaven and your own hell by your thoughts. Go within and find peace. You are immortal and you will never die. When you meditate, whatever is unnecessary will fall by the periphery. Whatever is important will take center stage. Turn within, look within.

You are a triune being and a self-manifestation of Consciousness. Everything is initiated from Consciousness with movements made out of the stuff of infinite possibilities. Its existence and power are Absolute in itself. Consciousness is One that manifests in multiplicity. It varies in soul-form but not in soul-essence. If Consciousness is the Source and is collective, then subtle, which makes up the mental and the vital, is the diffused illumination of Consciousness into your soul which would now begin to individualize in its descent into the gross physical body and is a part of your transcendent world, not the physical world. It is also the over-arching commander of the vital force which is also in the subtle body. The vital body is where your feelings and emotions are stored and out of which the morphogenetic field operates and moves energy. The physical is the gross body and follows suit from the vital body. When all of your bodies drop off, Consciousness is! Your implicate order is primary. You, however, have come out of the Divine, and you shall return to the Divine. You are an eternal harmony with numberless notes. In the meanwhile, however, ask yourself how you must change in order to arrive at your true nature as a self-multiplied Identical, uninvaded by death and birth. Begin now. Be patient. Everything in its appointed time.

The energy from your different levels trickle from the top down and not from the bottom up as Newtonian physics has erroneously informed and on which much of our culture has been built. Your different levels are also immune to time and space except for the physical. Time and space are a product of your third dimensional world and not of the fourth or fifth dimensional world. Your Consciousness is very dynamic and not a fixed or static thing. Communication amongst your various subtle levels can happen instantly without a visible linear pathway. A large quantum sudden non-sequential jump, discontinuity, can occur with non-local signals amongst your various dimensions to result in a swift and instantaneous spiritual resolution. In the descriptive sense, the levels of Consciousness are all different. In the dynamic sense, your levels are one despite that they are fifth and fourth dimension except for your physical body which is third dimension. They each have a life of their own with varying degrees of vitality but they are all interconnected.

TOUCHED BY THE FLAME OF LIGHT

In November of 1990, I had a very large non-sequential non-linear jump in my spirituality which had a profound effect on my beliefs and life purpose. I directly experienced the circle from which the Infinite radiates. It is this experience that fully opened my eyes to the limitations of orthodoxy and led me to begin exploring the interdimensional concepts of the life cycle since the experience left me longing for its essence.

In 1990, I was visiting a friend when I felt like I faded out of sight and out of consciousness. I was immersed into a vortex of Light of a very different frequency vibration, floating and traversing into a different dimension, and witnessing immense displays of fractal fireworks. I was suspended in this state. For how long I do not know as there was no sense of time and space in this Light experience. Where was my soul being carried off? I had no conscious part in this play. It was as if a huge tidal wave lifted my soul swiftly. I do not know if I was out of the body; but what I do know is that I was in a different space from which I typically live. In this Light I felt total stillness and joy. I felt whole and integrated and needed nothing. I was in awe at the sense of oneness and unity of it all. I experienced a heightened sense of perception as it transported me beyond the restrictions of my limited self-concept to a connection with something Greater than my third dimensional self. I was being shifted from the well-known to the ineffable. This noetic experience was the highest kind of state-of-grace I could possibly conceive and live. The sense of integration was beyond description.

This experience with the Light world occurred during the moment I was receiving Communion as I was in the office of a priest friend. Even though I had left the Catholic Church by many years, I still had a special affinity and awe with the Host. My priest friend favored me with this gift, as he was not one to be bound by orthodoxy. It was in the midst of receiving the Host that the Light experience unfolded. There were no words exchanged, only the numinous experience of the Light.

I do not know on what merit I received this gift because it arrived unannounced and certainly unrequested. I was overcome with the wonder of the Light. I was exploding with a high voltage current of energy! Filled with the Light of Consciousness, I *knew* the truth that "I am perfect!" In the flames of this Light, all conditioning was burned away and I felt a Divine intention wrapped up in this divine gift. I would never think of myself as separate again. The illusion of separateness was destroyed. I now *knew* there was no more differentiation between the inner and outer world. I was filled with awe and ecstasy through this spiritual radiance. This Light experience was a profound epiphany for me which illuminated my spiritual path. It shocked me out of my established system of beliefs because the realness of other dimensions was very convincing. It has made me more attentive to never be careless and "miss the mark' as I never want to be separated from this Majestic Light for which I yearn to this very day. An astounding depth of insight seemed to have exploded within me. It quickened me and alerted me to higher spiritual values and a much closer relationship with Spirit. I was profoundly changed by this unexpected journey to the beyond as it broke my former patterns of thought. I became more spiritually oriented and asserted other perspectives. The radically altering effects of this mystical experience left me with a firm conviction of the immortality of our human soul and with very little interest in material possessions.

Yet words fail to convey the grandeur of this experience. I was forever thrust into a quantum mode of thinking and being that had a deeply influential effect on my life and my career. Its effects have been long-lasting. Separateness ceased to exist. I *knew* instantly the ground is always one. It is also this experience that cemented my view on the harmfulness that orthodoxy continues to have on our collective human unconscious.

I instantaneously adapted to the Light world and did not want to leave. Yet, I felt myself being forced back into my encapsulated body and back to the earth world. I was bewildered by having been returned to myself. I resisted and I objected with the power of my soul. Yet, I was returned with my expanded Self funneled back into a constricted self. I moaned and wept for an hour wrapped up like a fetus on the office floor of my friend for the "loss" of the Light world. Tears flowed in abundance. I seemed to have died temporarily only to give more life to my soul. It is as if Source said, "Now this soul is Mine. Let no one touch it!"

For six months subsequent to this movement of my soul, I felt like a Martian on planet earth. I was unable to adapt to the lower vibration since now my frequency vibration was significantly elevated. My brain seemed to be reconfiguring itself as I was being tuned to other functional frequencies. I was no longer satisfied with anything less than the Light world. I wanted to remain a soul in ecstasy. I felt asleep to anything outside myself and unable to understand anything that did not lead to this awakening again. I only felt relief with my interior Self. I would meditate for hours in hope to catch the tiniest glimpse of the Light world. I wanted to get rid of everything that was an obstacle to this solitude. This vision left such an impression, that all I wanted was to experience it again. Many small sparks would shimmer and course around me. I wanted to go back so as to eliminate my spiritual torment. I could hardly endure any further delays. Nothing on the outside any longer satisfied me. My earth wings were clipped. No more illusions. The spiritual pain from not being in the Light world was unbearable.

I became overwhelmed with the meaninglessness of our materialistic civilization and the emptiness of our ritualistic activities. Through this mystical state of deep insight, I was never more awake in the things of Spirit. I felt transformed in a dramatic way by this transcendent energy. Nothing on this earth has ever had the same significance. This was a pure moment of ecstasy with the spiritual world, the heavenly inner realms. I could only be consoled momentarily through meditation where I was able to glimpse this deep Source within myself. I felt greedy for this vision to return. A dormant force seemed to have been awakened and became active. I experienced a spiritual awakening by grace where I understood more than I saw of our spiritual cosmic holomovement. The more you use these gifts the more you produce. You never use them up.

I continued to feel detached from the earth world, still oscillating at a higher pitch for many months, while my soul remained in ecstasy. I viewed the earth life from afar as if on a screen and feeling separate from it. I could clearly see the thick layers of ignorance on the earth world filled with barren experiences. This experience with the Light created a discontinuous non-sequential jump into my spirituality as all impressions of the past were wiped out. It produced a very rapid, qualitative shift, a lasting change in consciousness itself, altering the perception of myself and the world. It filled me with peace, mental clarity, and serenity once I was able to re-establish myself in an oscillating manner more common to the earth world. It took me more than six months to reach this state and to objectify the experience of transcendency. Everything became colored with a different paint brush, the brush of Light, the experience with the Void. It became clear that Infinite Intelligence descends to us through his embodiment in our physical nature, and then we must rise and ascend back to Source. We return Home because only the Void is real and the nonvoid, the material transitory world, is illusory. It is your conditioned perceptions that keep you from experiencing the Void. These conditioned perceptions keep you from seeing higher frequency domains. You will perceive the seamless wholeness of the Void in meditation as you will have a direct nonconceptual experience of the undifferentiated whole of the experiencer and the experienced.

The memory of the rapture of such a numinous event still remains. All I want is to be saturated in this Consciousness of Light. The Light spread through my body and forever dwells in my heart. Since then I have learned and understood that the Light is not somewhere else. It is within me. I temporarily lost my human form. We are each a self-referenced cosmology. This inner divine power is within each of us. This Light constitutes but a narrow portion of a vast, continuous electromagnetic spectrum that resides within us. This stupendous and ineffable moment with the implicate world awakened a new phase of spiritual development for me. It has been the gateway to many more spiritual experiences that come from the flowing out and in from our primary vital essence. Everything returns to the impersonal unknown.

After this numinous experience, I began to depend only on my inner state because it is the awareness of our own divinity that is missing in most of us. We forget the knowledge of our bodies. That is all that mattered. Stop staggering blindly on the road to nowhere where you will be met by a big empty hole. Thirst for the non-dualistic experience of your inner Self. Let everything else fade into the periphery and find out for yourself how you can enlighten yourself in a split second.

Shortly after this mystical experience, a book was channeled through me, another unsolicited gift, entitled The Spiritual Dance Of Life *Where Two Worlds Meet,* which examines how you can reach deeper levels of Consciousness for your healing. The experience with the Light world was a high voltage guidance for the inspiration of this book which reflects and instructs how spiritual experiences are multi-dimensional. It is this book, which had been seen and read by the Director of the Institute of Mental Health and Neurology in Bangalore, India during a visit to America while he was visiting a friend in Chicago, that then led to an invitation to speak at the Institute's international conference on hypnosis and past lives. You can see the chain of events and synchronicities.

The Spiritual Dance of Life played a transformative role with the players of a particular court case. Two decades ago I had been retained as a consultant in a very messy custody case. My evaluation supported the plaintiff. The attorney for the defendant apparently researched my background and brought into the court proceedings the book, The Spiritual Dance of Life. It was also apparent that he read the book thoroughly. However, his use of the book in the proceedings was to discredit me as an expert witness in front of the judge and jury. He quoted extensively from the book during the three-hour interrogation peppered by rapid inquires of me about the book while on the witness stand. I was unruffled. I did ask the attorney what this book had to do with this case. He said, "I want to know how you think." I responded, "I think very well thank you." The jury and the judge laughed out loud! He interrogated roughly, "Is rebirth the same as reincarnation?" I responded, "They are both states where non-physical essences initiate a new life for their progressive evolution." He then asked me if I believed in reincarnation. I responded in the affirmative and told him that I even believed in Santa Claus.

Once the court proceedings were over, this attorney (I assumed he was around age fifty-five) came to me and asked if he might speak to me privately. I stood there ready and receptive to whatever he had to say. He declared, "I am a very bad guy. I am not a nice guy of an attorney. I am trying to be a nice guy these last couple of years and I am telling you this because I want you to hear and believe what I am going to say next to you. I love your book! I do not know whether I will have another life after this, but I very much like what you have to say in the book." He went on further, and I continued to listen without interruption. "I see an aura of kindness and naivete around you that I have never seen in a professional." Then his client, the defendant whom I did not support in the case, also walked over to me while his attorney was speaking with me. The defendant remarked, "I wish I knew you many years ago. I know you would have helped our marriage while no one else has been able to do so." At this point we all went home.

The next morning I received a phone call from the defendant's attorney. He again began commenting very favorably on the book The Spiritual Dance of Life after which point he asked me if I would be willing to accept referrals from him despite that he was based five hours away from my clinic. The moral of this story is that when we have strong convictions, in the darkest alley we can shine a light.

A few months ago, I had another Light experience mildly resembling the one in 1990 while doing energy work with a friend. While in a light trance state, a bolt of white light came shooting in me from the sky with unbelievable force. It struck the area between my eyebrows and continued onwards within me. The rapidly shooting light was approaching me with such speed and seeming force that I flinched. But no matter, as it followed its target between my eyebrows! It entered me. I cried out with great joy. An extraordinary moment! I became totally oblivious to what was happening in my external world. I retired my self into the universal Self. I was not conscious of my whereabouts or of my physical body. I drifted for what seemed an hour into a transcendental world having been totally unaware that the energy practitioner had signaled me by touching both my feet that we were done and verbally informed me we had concluded our work. I did not feel her nor hear her signals because I seemed to have entered the Void. I laid there in pure ecstasy resting in the tiny blue light, the Blue Pearl, the Light of Self, that appeared in my optical chakra, ajna. The Blue Pearl was drifting from sahasrara, the crown chakra, to ajna, the third eye chakra. It was sparkling and scintillating. It eventually filled my entire crown area. In this closed-eye vision, my eyelids felt as if they were glued together. I could not open them no matter how hard I tried. This was another marvelous process, another grace with which I was favored. From this experience, I was left with a feeling of detachment, a feeling of witnessing without involvement, a pulling back and listening with my soul. It enhanced new heights of already familiar ones. I developed a lack of expectation of what may need to develop in moment-to-moment living. How blessed am I to be reminded of what powerful and sensitive beings we are. I see the blue light, now, in everyone and realize that I am the light which spreads everywhere. The more you meditate, the more you learn the knack of stillness. Then you become a clean calm ocean that reflects the moon.

Each vision of universal connectedness facilitates many shifts as they uncover more and more of what orthodoxy seems to hide from us. My way of understanding the outside world continues to change as shifts take place in the energetic field of my brain. There is ample research that shows mystical experiences rewire neural impulses, some connections are weakened, and some others are strengthened between parts of the cerebrum. These shifts are sobering, and, at times, decentralizing as I keep being offered the choice repeatedly to further abandon old patterns and comfort zones.

My way of viewing my inner world becomes clearer as I surf through the red (gross body), white (subtle body), black (causal body) and blue lights (Consciousness) of the different layers of my spiritual body. These multiple visions started me on a spiritual quest of a different dimension. Through these experiences, I am more aware of how the mind can function and that spiritual insights and healings come from the depths of our Consciousness. Everything is now colored with a different paint brush, the brush of my experience with the Light World. The memory of the rapture of these mystical experiences still remains and has helped me know that the Light is not somewhere else. They have left their mark on me! The Light is within me.

What merit do I have to receive these graces through these mystical experiences which have created lasting transformations? These exceptional favors are indicators of Source's infinite goodness because each brings with it an experiential grasp of the Truth. No one is precluded. Nothing in this world has ever compared to the ecstasy of such experiences. These soul raptures pull me out of my senses. This is the Game of Life where nothing is an accident or a coincidence. Our experiences, including mystical experiences, are all synchronistic encounters to uncover how powerful we are under all the societal conditioning. Harvest the profound wisdom which comes from mystical experiences because it has the potential to heal the planet on a multidimensional level. Perhaps such ineffable experiences, available to all, and which push us past our limits, may be the path to global healing.

WE ARE HYBRID: LIVING IN TWO WORLDS SIMULTANEOUSLY

Your spirituality, therefore, can shift suddenly and permanently. Your spirituality and your healing need to be addressed from all levels. You are an alchemical marriage. Therefore, when you ignore the fourth and fifth dimension, the data you acquire is inadequate and inconclusive rendering any healing incomplete. Quantum living teaches "big spirituality" in that it teaches personal capacity, strength and power. Quantum living is always self-referencing. Explore the enormous expanse with which you were born.

Perhaps you are seeing slightly more clearly now how you live in two worlds simultaneously – the third dimensional physical world and the fourth dimensional spiritual world which are both propelled by the Force of Consciousness, the Causal body and fifth dimension. In this downward causation quantum spirituality model, the whole acts on all the different parts through a level-entanglement process where the whole has an effect over all your other levels. This process is only possible through the interconnections of your protons, electrons and neutrons, the wiring of your Consciousness. This is where your Consciousness (your hardware) takes a complex task and simplifies it by splitting it up into smaller modules through your supramental, mental and vital (your software) and feeds it until it gets to your base level, the physical (your computer monitor) where the majority of the visible work is done. You have a very rapid dynamic wireless communication system whose direction is guided by meaning and determines your dance. All the levels have to adapt through the process but this adaptation can be changed based on new information which you provide from your Central Regulator. That is why there is a hierarchal structural symbiosis between your hardware and your software. This is a relationship of reciprocal influence (quantum entanglement) which gives your system purpose and meaning derived from your highest level, Consciousness. Your lower levels are doing the work, but they are being influenced by your Consciousness – a top-down dynamic continuous flowing process. "Of myself I do nothing," instructed Jesus, "but the Father within does all things!" Therefore, the thoughts that come from your higher level (Consciousness, supramental and mental) affect your base levels (vital and physical) and cause your whole being to be in frequent recalibration. Perhaps you may not any longer want to adhere to cultural interpretations of who you are and who you can become.

Beware of the psychotic interpretations of life which many have imposed as the dominant interpretation of your life. Rather, walk through the doorway of your own integrity to support your evolution. Culture's hypnotic dogma renders you in a trance and is one of disempowerment and limitations. You can choose to be a victim of life or the creator of your life. The choice you make will determine the level of spiritual evolution you will experience. Quantum spirituality empowers you while orthodox thinking keeps you subordinate to its hierarchy. You are not a larva. You are a butterfly. Test your wings. Begin a new life.

The higher levels of Consciousness slow down their vibrations to allow for the collapse into the physical base level. At the base linear level, the tasks have been simplified into simple operations. Yet it is very difficult to explain through lower-level behaviors the activities of the multi-fold causation in the higher hierarchy because the linear concepts do not apply to the non-linear behavior. All the levels which are strongly bound internally interact together to make sure the desired outcome is achieved. These are the reasons it is so important that you do not merely focus on the physical for your spiritual evolution or healing because the physical is subordinate and is not a singular cause. Rather, look at the web of influences that can aid you in your overall development. When you look at a spiritual position, you can then see different levels of meaning in your ideology. You cannot derive this type of highly sophisticated spiritual information from the orthodox model because it is confined to the base level. Therefore, you will not have sufficient conditions nor higher end possibilities because of its limitations. Your spiritual evolution must happen at your level of Consciousness and the gate of entry is meditation. When you reach this level, the physical/material world will become a meaningless nothing as you revel in total bliss. Bring order from all this chaos with which you have been conditioned. You are the producer, writer and creator of your life. Wake up. There is a better way to live.

QUANTUM ENTANGLEMENT

Quantum entanglement has to become understood and appreciated in spirituality. When you fail to act as a unit with the Supreme One, you become dysfunctional. This is where you "miss the mark." This is the agony of your soul. This is your hell! Orthodoxy dictates what you will do, you bow your head, and you just listen. Quantum spirituality wants a discernible link between you and Infinite Creative Source for collaborative work. There is no higher or lower level. Movement goes back and forth between Infinite Intelligence and you, to allow for a leap in spiritual healing by returning you to the starting point, the original level – Oneness – by being with you in the collective. Both blend and become one with each other so that the two of you create an oscillation of vibration and an intense relational space by synchronizing your nervous system with that of Consciousness. This communal nonlinear vibration is now highly ordered and inseparable and creates a more precise attunement. You highlight one another and extrapolate from the different perspectives. In quantum spirituality you "think as God thinks" as the Sufis say, to bring about a dramatic change by plugging into the electromagnetic source of Infinite Intelligence. This is a dynamic movement of energies, a quantum entanglement. You build a bridge with Consciousness by calibrating vibrations for a reciprocal flow of energy. You do not barricade yourself by some invisible pretentious wall of orthodoxy. Rather, open yourself up to quantum entanglement by going into your silence. When you touch your inner sovereignty, no pretense is necessary. This will jumpstart you out of your limitations and spiritual emptiness. Then Source can be the eyes through which you will begin to see the physical world. This unification with Consciousness will become like a pendulum, by downplaying one level and highlighting another. You extrapolate from these different levels and shift from one perspective, the human, to another, the Divine. The merger creates a resonance because "there is nothing on earth that does not have its correspondence at the super-celestial level or the Divine Treasury," instructs Sufi Master Pir Vilayat Inayat Khan. This resonance will allow you to see your beliefs in a different light, undo the imbalance which has been creating so much of your stress, and create space for a different form, quantum spirituality.

Quantum entanglement will shape your spiritual relationship. Quantum entanglement takes into consideration that the separation with which you have been indoctrinated is illusory. Quantum entanglement is a unitary experience of two energies and becomes a self-referencing experience from which limitless spiritual healing will take place. However, growth can be lonely, because once you awaken from your present hypnotic trance, many others will still be asleep. I experienced this profound loneliness after my sudden transcendent mystical experience in 1990. I no longer had a common language with the people on planet earth and communication was difficult. I felt displaced. I went into my silence as I did not want to become a missionary for others. I continued to cultivate my own inner growth. I knew then there was a better way to live.

Awaken to your own multidimensional nature. Awaken to self-Consciousness and project yourself into quantum spirituality to make rapid spiritual evolution possible and visible. Unfoldment is in your own hands and it is important to stay awake to the evolutionary forces within. One is the fruit and the seed is hidden within. Nature is patient and is waiting for self-recognition. Move yourself from the larva to the butterfly stage. Move from Homo Sapiens to Homo Spiritualis with the sudden change in perspective awakening to the transcendental dimension. Quantum entanglement sits on the premise that separation then is an illusion. Spatio-temporal limitations of self are optical illusions!

ON A CLEAR DAY, YOU CAN SEE FOREVER

One day, as my husband and I returned home in early evening, I became suddenly aware of an internal shift. The sense of well-being and joy which I had experienced throughout the day, suddenly dissipated into one of internal alarm and hyper-alertness. There was suddenly a sense of intense urgency and emergency. I knew that someone was in grave danger. There was a diffuse but absolutely compelling direction toward a friend, Stephen, whose family I had met during one of my speaking engagements in Australia. I sat in meditation in expectant silence asking, "What is happening right now?" and made sure that I could be with it whatever it was.

I had not seen Stephen and his family for years. Stephen lived across the pond in another continent! I sat in Deep Silence. Through this Silence, I felt compelled to telephone Stephen and relate my sudden, spontaneous and intrinsically guided but alarming experience. I asked him if he was okay. I cautioned him that he may be in some danger. He had been at work all day, and his day had been uneventful he reported. Later in the day, however, I received a return call from Stephen. As Stephen left a stock exchange workshop in which he was a speaker, and walked to his vehicle to return home to his wife and children, he found his car broken into, his computer stolen, passports missing, and several documents of intellectual property had disappeared as well. On his laptop was a series of critical medical databases, intellectual property contracts, companies' correspondence, patent details and other significant information which had not been recently backed up on a secure drive.

The loss was devastating to Stephen, but in its own way a serious "wake-up call," he stated. Stephen related that for the first time Providence had shown him what it feels like to have a loss that cannot be reversed. "Short of permanent physical harm how else can we feel the poignancy of an irreversible event?" he inquired. Stephen recognized the need to tidy up his life and to do things in a timely fashion as sometimes there are no second chances. "We can kid ourselves," Stephen added, "that there is a fallback position we can take that will minimize our loss, but sometimes when the boom drops, there is no going back."

Stephen still carried anger over this unfortunate incident as he expounded, "One of the aspects of the incident that still causes me anger is the collective damage that is caused by the self-absorption of someone with a drug habit." Apparently, he was informed by police authorities that it looked like the work of habitual drug users. "In order to meet some transient feeling of pleasure or relief, they have no compunction about causing a major dislocation to someone else. We are powerless against that level of total disregard," Stephen added further.

That same night my clairvoyant remote viewing experience continued. I kept seeing a crowbar in my dream. I feared Stephen was still in danger and not out of the woods yet. I reached out to Stephen again by telephone and inquired about this iron bar that had kept appearing during dreamtime. Stephen related to me that the thieves had used a thin metal bar, with one sharp edge, down the inside of his car window to pop open the lock. The metal bar was a foot long and made from steel rulers filed down to a long narrow "V" with a sharp edge for slashing. This instrument was similar to the old-fashioned stiletto knife. This clairvoyant experience is a clear example which reveals our all-knowing mind. On a clear day you can see forever.

You can see now the importance of exploring methods that allow access to the innate power and endless knowledge that lies dormant within each of us. Going into your Circle of Silence is a method of communicating with the collective unconscious and for accessing fourth dimensional levels of consciousness toward your spiritual emergence. Energy is nonlocal. Time and distance have no effect. Energy exists everywhere all the time. We are all related through the web of unseen forces.

"Science may have defined life too small. If we continue to

define life too small, we will define ourselves too small as well," remarks Rachel Naomi Remen, M.D. who left a lucrative medical post because she could no longer do medicine in the way that she was taught. How often and how deeply these nonlocal experiences occur is not the issue, but how you will allow them to influence your life matters. It does require a type of heroism in your disposition to confront and explore the full range of all that you can be, the full range of all your available experiences. On a mentally clear day, you can see forever.

UTTER STILLNESS AND EXPECTANT SILENCE

Wait without thought for you are not ready for thought.
So the darkness shall be light and the stillness the dancing
Alan Watts

Stop your chatter and get beyond your whirlpool of thoughts. Speak only when absolutely necessary! Communicate on a deeper level because it is only in the depth of silence that you will cleanse your perceptions and find infinity. I do not have the vocabulary through verbal language to describe the ecstasy of silence. It makes me want to be occupied in things that benefit my soul. It is so beyond description because as you close your outer eyes you open your inner eye and listen to the whisper of your soul. Then your whole being becomes your eye with which you see the world. Actively engage with silence, a space where you find inner stillness and peace. This is where you begin to see with your inner eyes and hear with your inner ears. It is a space full of tranquility, equilibrium and harmony here. The longer you stay in the silence, the more you become absorbed into the Silence. This is where you will enjoy a deeper state of serenity. Eventually you disappear into the Silence as you bathe yourself in the total stillness. Listen for wisdom to come from your own inner voice. This is a divine occasion because there is nowhere to go and nothing to do but listen to your own inner wisdom. This is your new beginning filled with the power of mystical potential. In this silence you will find how worthy you are of great honor and how magnificent you are as a child of the Light. Stop hiding your divinity the same way that cataracts blur your vision. Remove the veil, remove the screen. Are you ready to learn something beyond that with which you have grown accustomed?

Silence often conjures memories of my time in the Himalayas

when I was invited to speak during the month of November on hypnosis at the National Institute of Mental Health and Neurological Sciences (Institute of Neurology) in Bangalore in the southern part of India. While there, I felt an irresistible current draw me to northern India to hike the majestic Himalayan Mountains. The unforgiving bitter winds and jagged peaks of the mountains are just commanding. The silence is haunting and remains in memory and consciousness and not quickly forgotten. The Himalayas bow my head to nature and to Spirit! It is an untouched and undefeated part of our world. In these mystical mountains full of wonder and mystery is where the gods descend from heaven to walk among the snowy peaks of the Himalayas. The incredible panoramic majesty of the mountains, of the hidden valleys and isolated peaks, was breathtaking. My very soul was lost in the sheer magnitude of the beauty before me despite losing electricity every day in early evening. I quickly learned to navigate my way in my room through candlelight. There was incredible physical beauty unlike any other that I had seen. This is where the pranic current is highly charged from the footsteps of the sages, and the energy vibrates very rapidly because it is pure here and has not been contaminated by various pollutions unlike many other parts of India. I found it to be the perfect place to merge my mind with the universe in a perfect ecstatic union. This was clearly a sacred moment in my ordinary life, a moment of great expansion in my awareness.

This spiritual journey to the foothills of the Himalayas felt hauntingly familiar. I couldn't help feel I had been here before. I pondered on these majestic mountains and the many seekers of truth who come from all over the world to pray and meditate and how they forged a connection with my life. An overwhelming tide of emotions surged within me. I wondered what historical nexus and node I fitted into. What is my connection between these majestic mountains and my soul? Everything seemed illuminated. I was seized with the feeling of extraordinary experience knowing that this is the heart and soul of the top of the world – the majestic Himalayan mountains – the mystical Himalayas as the locals call it. During those weeks in India, I lived in a strange and shifting rhythm and in an utterly transformed state. Everything around me seemed enchanted. I kept reciting the Buddha's Bhaddakaratta Sutra, *"Do not pursue the past. Do not lose yourself in the future. Looking deeply at life as it is in this very moment, the meditator dwells in stability and freedom!"* This moment matters.

While in India, one of my hosts, a former lieutenant in the Army of India, took me to chat with a spiritual Master. The spiritual Master informed me very quickly in our conversation that during this life time "you will experience self-realization." Rudely I laughed out loud asserting, "You must have me confused with someone else. I have so much work to do!" He continued to shake his head from side to side which for Indians means "yes" and I kept laughing and protesting. In 1997 I had not yet evolved into the understanding of self-realization. But now I know it to mean that in comparison to the bliss of the perennial knowledge that we acquire, everything appears and feels worthless compared to it. Self-realization is the absence of ignorance. It is about realizing the soul. I have stopped laughing as I have learned what I am not. I feel full. I need nothing.

I have spent a lifetime in search of my spiritual self which became displaced in my unconscious as social convention, psychological theoretical assumptions through fourteen years of academic training, and cultural language stripped my spirit. In this search, I learned to move from the old structures into a new paradigm with the primary authoritative guidance coming from my own voice. I learned slowly that I either drink from my own "spiritual well" or die! Since then I have passed through many struggles in attaining a certain balance in the equation of my life's purpose, and, of course, my life's objectives. Every "struggle" has moved me toward Spirit.

You can find Spirit in the world of everyday activities as readily as anywhere else. Let every movement carry you Godward. In the ordinary is where you will meet the sacred. It is the ordinary that will peak your states of consciousness, expand your awareness and become a powerful force for social change. Desire to learn to use your ordinary experiences and your difficulties to befriend spirit, and awaken heart – then have a passion to plumb to your soul's full extent - - right now! Life rushes onward like a roaring stream and drowns our thoughts in its noise. However, these unforgettable moments have marked themselves in golden pen upon the calendar of my years!

In Silent communication you can transcend the three-dimensional world of every day experience and realize a higher dimensional reality. There is absolutely nothing that a mirror could ever do to attract the sun but, in its stillness, and brightness, the sun attracts and nourishes everything. A highly spiritual colleague of mine said to me directly one time, "You are like the sun, Teri. All you have to do is merely appear and be there. Some people are nourished by the sun and some people are burned by the sun because they are not prepared to receive its nourishment. But it is not the fault of the sun." It is also your choice what you achieve out of your utter stillness. Through it you can prepare your mind to connect with the Divine, the Light will shine brightly within you, and you will dissolve all boundaries. In Silence you have the opportunity to break through the barriers that keep you chained to your old world of conditioning if you abandon your self to your Self.

How do you access your inner life? By moving inward gradually rather than living on the surface of life. Inner silence guides, illumines and directs you. In this silence is where you will release all negative emotions that clog up your heart and your cells. In this silence you will begin to loosen any crystallized emotions that have imbalanced your organs, your muscles and your tissues. Inward is where you will find your subtle self which is in constant communication with Consciousness. This will help you to widen the limits of your physical self and will begin your ascent. You will begin to feel expanded and eventually you will merge fully with Infinite Intelligence. You will become luminous as your body recalibrates with every movement of consciousness. This will be the making of your spiritual transformation. This is where you will find truth rather than falsehoods. Your healing process must begin at the spiritual level and through meditation you will be inspired from within. You will find your own way intuitively rather than relying on the opinions of others. Then you will move into service through action inspired by dynamic inner silence. Meditation will take you into the deepest levels of your Consciousness and aid you in manifesting your divine Source. There is nothing beyond Consciousness. All is within you. There is only you. Your Inner Self will guide you.

Let us dive into that Silence through meditation because meditation is an organic unfoldment from the lateral world of fiction. It awakens your consciousness by strengthening your electromagnetic field allowing you to be more present to your relationships and to deal more effectively with life and its challenges. Meditation is not about quieting the mind, but finding the quiet that is already within you. Just for today, quiet that internal dialogue and just be grateful.

QUANTUM MEDITATION
- WHERE DO I BEGIN

Meditation is your rehabilitation clinic because it allows you to heal in the quantum by transforming the cellular and chemical workings of your brain. Through quantum meditation you enter the universal mind, where a limitless power resides, and life will be experienced differently because you will recalibrate yourself to higher frequencies with every breath you take. No physical manipulation of your physical body just breath work that shifts you away from the beta state of brainwave activity. It is simple, powerful, profound and an atomic accelerator which broadens your focus into infinite absolute reality. It is a way of connecting to the healing energy of your inner body so you may heal the underlying source of sickness not mere physical symptoms. It is a spiritual medicine to cure your inner life and your outer life. It will bring you to a place of inner stillness and grace, and transcend your third dimensional matrix, balance your central and entheric nervous system, and help you ascend. You will shift into a dimensionally larger world with a much higher frequency and raise the vibratory tone of your entire body. Quantum meditation is your door to great healing. Quantum meditation will help you to see the false as false, which eventually becomes your natural state of being, and you will be charged with a new Light and vigor. It is a heightened state of concentrated awareness which will help you blossom into your fifth dimensional nature. It will teach you to call on the higher dimensions of your being because there is an enormous potential that lies dormant within each one of us.

Quantum meditation will bring about both acute and long-term changes in your brain and bodily functions. The fourth and seventh chakra are both deeply affected in a deep state of quantum meditation. The rhythm of the heart changes with every cycle of your breath. The vibrational waves of daily practice of meditation will create many additional changes in the central nervous system. Quantum meditation is not something you do; rather, it is something you grow toward. It is a living relationship with the infinite power that surrounds and inhabits you. Begin somewhere. Grope in your darkness to find your door. My words are not a formula, but a doorknob in your darkness. Perhaps keep groping and decide if you want to reach for the door.

Quantum meditation is a way of accessing the data in the integrative data base of your SuperComputer. In the receptive stance of meditation you will become more receptive to the dynamic part of yourself and you will become endowed to attract whatever you desire. This may seem difficult at first, but actually all you are doing is going back to your true nature. You will feel a calmness descend upon you and an opening. Meditative devotion develops naturally through practice as it assists you in feeling increasingly in touch with your whole being.

Quantum meditation is an intensely relaxing and alert state that links your mind and body through breath work. Breath is the first thing you do when you come to planet earth and the last physical act you will do when you leave planet earth. Practiced daily, quantum meditation will help you to transition at the highest vibration of yourself. It is the most important and simple activity you do all day that connects to life itself. Your breath is your direct link to subtle energy. It is truly your Life Force.

Quantum meditation will help take the lens of illusion away from your inner sight. It will clear your lens of your spiritual cataracts. You will become an artist of sacredness through meditation and you will no longer wander in illusion. Meditation will provide you with the psychic fuel to become a spiritual athlete and explore the minefield of your mind in a boundless process of existence. Every effort will open up the peep hole of your mind through which the Light can shine. Meditation is a sacred technology that assists you in becoming the curator of your spirit by helping you dive into the vastness of the Ocean of Consciousness. Through meditation you will bring this Consciousness right into your being. When you feel this power coming from your higher dimensions, others around you will feel it right away. You will become magnetic so that others will want to be around you because meditation aids in increasing your magnetic field. Turn within! You will radiate. Do not keep that radiancy to yourself. Cast it out through your eyes, and through your third eye, like a beam straight to others. Then always wear a millionaire smile! Meditation keeps you strong, and others can never dominate you where you are strong.

The biggest and most important transformation you will experience through quantum meditation is that you will attain the knowledge that your essence within you is Infinite Source and that this is also your place of origin. Quantum meditation is a gateway to a special kind of self-knowledge that will show you how powerful your beliefs can be when originated from your Silence. It is an inner-world adventure into the inner frontiers of Consciousness. It is a homeopathic move to go mentally with what is always an inherent and available attribute of mankind. In quantum meditation your mind will expand and encourage you to look at principles operating beyond the common view. You will achieve levels of your psyche for your healing not reached through normal activities of your consciousness. This is the quantum life tied into the neuroplasticity of the body. This attainment will then strengthen all your activities in the physical world. Your other choice is to continue to suffer in the delusion of duality which clouds your path.

Let us have an experience of, rather than a conversation about, quantum meditation. Sit in a quiet spot on a chair with your spine erect or lie down. Breath is different when you are lying down and it is easy to drift into sleep. I strongly recommend sitting. Set your spine as straight as an arrow with your spinal vertebrae stacked one on top of another. Important to not be tilting your head backwards, sideways or forward, but in line with your spine. Keep it all relaxed and tension free. Sit light, not heavy. Sit easy, not hard. Lower your shoulders away from your ears. Posture is a most important component of meditation. Stabilize your posture. Your spine needs to be straight as an arrow as well if you choose to lie down to meditate. Breathe from your belly button, from your third chakra (manipura), not from your upper chest. Feel the subtle movements of your breath. Meditate on an empty stomach, otherwise, your body is busy digesting and will not allow you to get into a relaxed state. If you need to eat, then wait two hours for the food to digest and meditate afterwards. However, if the hunger-monkey is chasing you, then eat something small and light, or take a glass of juice, and then meditate.

Place your hands softly on your lap with palms up so you are in a receptive mode with the right palm on top of the left palm with thumbs touching forming a circle. Create a closed circuit so your energy becomes circular and not thrown out from any point. Breathe from your belly and breathe effortlessly. Inhale/exhale/inhale/exhale. Inhale and exhale from your nose, effortlessly. Follow the sensations of your breath. Feel that breath running through your nostrils. Uncross your arms and legs. Ground your feet to the floor if you are sitting. Lower and relax your shoulders and your face. Relax and let them go.

Breathing has a calming effect especially as it naturally slows down with increased practice. Breathe from your navel from where you originated. Let's go back to your roots. The more you live from this center, the navel, the more alive you will feel.

As you breathe in, the oxygen is passing into your bloodstream to oxygenate every cell and tissue of your body from the in-breath. However, know you are not just drawing oxygen from the atmosphere and releasing toxic gases. You are, rather, plugging your electromagnetic field into the electromagnetic field of the Infinite Universe. The in-breath is also the first breath you take when you come on planet earth. On the in-breath, you come back home. As you breathe in, feel yourself expanding into your unlimitedness. Breathe in Light, Light, Light. As you exhale, you release waste gases such as carbon dioxide from your lungs to leave the bloodstream. Breathe out all imbalances and impurities from your physical body. Wherever you feel disquietude in your body, breathe into it and breathe out all your excess baggage. Let your breath flow naturally. Be calm. Be still.

The inhale is the feminine receptive breath associated with the left side of the body and the exhale is the masculine emissive breath and also associated with the right side of the body. The last breath you take as you leave planet earth is the exhalation symbolic of letting go of everything external. This last breath is how you detach from the physical when you transition. However, know that you do not die. You existed infinitely before you had your present body, and you will continue to exist after you drop your present body. It is a very interesting place you will enter once you drop your physical body because you will travel into a nonlinear field and be able to accomplish things you could not do in your physical body. It is like the metamorphosis of the caterpillar into the butterfly who gives up his encapsulated body and can then fly unbounded. This life cycle is certainly not the end, as we keep going from soul-plane to soul-plane.

It is important that you balance your breaths, otherwise, you overload one over the other and throw your energetic system out of balance. This balanced breathing will help you to return to harmony. Continue to breathe, effortlessly, as you connect to this life energy field and amp up your electromagnetic voltage.

Remember that breath is the most important thing you do all day. It is the first thing you do when you come on planet earth. It is the last thing you will do as you leave planet earth. It is truly your life force. Outside of meditation, you take twelve to twenty breaths per minute. In meditation, you will take two to five breaths per minute as you slow down breath, you manage it, you direct it, effortlessly.

Now go inward. Let us find your peace within. Allow space where language does not exist. It is a growing process that grows and expands. Just exist without words. Language dulls your life because it is repetitive and boring. The more you make language and talking important to you, the more boredom you will experience in life because words keep you on the surface. Such communication never becomes communion. Stop killing the moment with your old language. The moment you speak you divide yourself from the other. Only in silence are you One. By focusing on your breath, you will get away from distracting thoughts. The only thing between you and meditation are words. Your breath will provide a single point of reference into the silence. Take a deep breath and release it into silent surrender, effortlessly. Be aware that you are breathing in. Be with the silence and be silently present to your breath. Be fully absorbed in it, effortlessly. Feel the way silence feels. Let that deep silence fill your every breath. Let it dance you. Let your body breathe you! Stay inwardly self-focused. Go deeper yet. Exhale and breathe out and be aware that you are breathing out. Breathe effortlessly into your silence. Concentrate every atom of your body on your breath, on your silence. The mind needs to breathe in order to think. As you go into silence, slow down breath, then thinking slows or stops. Remember that you are an energetic being of love and light. This silence is an investment that grows.

Your mind is like a drunken monkey going from one branch of thought to another. If you receive a divine thought, breathe it into your Self and grow it. Divine thoughts have the potential to shift you into a higher realm. If you receive a negative thought, either release it through the top of your head or remind yourself that fish at the top of the ocean cannot disturb the vast depths of the calm tranquil ocean. Feel yourself as the bottom of the sea, calm, and quiet. Then no play of thought has the potential to disturb you without your permission like fish in the sea that jump up and down at the surface of the water but leave no ripple in the depths of the vast ocean. You are that Ocean.

Go even deeper into your silence. When there is no language, you enter the Void, the non-verbal existence of the common tongue. Let silence breathe you in stillness so that what was once impossible becomes possible, effortlessly. Let go and let silence fill your heart with Light. Begin to listen to your heart the way silence listens. Silence is One. Let your heart speak only the truth. Be open in the heart and feel for intuitive guidance. See it open fully. Let yourself just be. Inhale/exhale/inhale/exhale – effortlessly – as you tune yourself to a different pitch. Stay aware that you are breathing in and out. Pause between each in and out breath. Breathe in infinity; breathe out the external world. With your breath you will touch the Divine Spark within you in your silence. Let your breath tune you into pure serenity. Let it dance you – effortlessly. Breathe – effortlessly. Let this silence fill your heart, breath and body. Let go – effortlessly. Keep observing your breath as it flows in and out – effortlessly.

With your eyes closed, look at the point between your eyebrows as if you are looking at the top of a mountain. This is your third eye center (ajna), the seat of Consciousness. Now feel this beautiful connection from the third eye to the heart – up and down, up and down, up and down – a continual act of giving and receiving. Keep following your breaths. Important to open up the fourth heart chakra simultaneously as you open the third eye chakra. Stay with this movement between the heart and the third eye. Keep this dynamic movement softly in focus. Tune in as this is where you will receive intuitive insights toward your evolution. From this space is where you will function with clarity and vision and learn how to navigate through an illness by adding light to those areas of imbalance. From this space you will learn to access your inner healer who will guide the regeneration of your body.

Now chant mentally, "I AM" as you focus on ajna, your third eye. Chant mentally "I" when you inhale and chant "AM" when you exhale. This mantra is your operator's and maintenance manual all in your own soul. Chant in silence and connect with that timeless Spirit. Now finally settle in on ajna, your third eye chakra, and contemplate at this point, no movement, just exist in it deep inside you.

Silence is indefinable. Abstract Truth can only be experienced in silence and not through words which are mere representations of Truth. Silence is pure potentia so you can collapse karma. "I AM" will stabilize your concentration. You will become peaceful. Focus on the gaps – the silence. You will eventually become the "I Am" and at that point all mantras will drop naturally. They will no longer be needed. You will learn through meditation that you are sufficient unto yourself.

Always stay focused on your breath. Relax in each breath. Your breath will take you into Eternity, a time of perpetual movement.

All is Consciousness! Stay in silence and keep breathing – effortlessly. Now take one last deep breath and with your own biorhythm and at your own speed, slowly, gently open your eyes. Never rush out of meditation. Let your body tell you when it is time to open your eyes. Your gains will vary in direct proportion to your practice. Meditation will improve your overall well-being. Your application has to be unrelenting if you want to experience that Everything is Consciousness! However, having provided this structure on meditation, do not get stuck in the structure as it is only a prototype to get you started. What is important is the life it animates.

I often like to finish my meditations by chanting: *Ong Namo, Guru Dev, Namo* (I bow to my Highest Consciousness). I then follow with: *Wahe Guru* (out of darkness into the Light). I chant because I know that chanting affects my energetic body on many levels. It also self-generates my energy.

Mantras such as "I AM" transport you into a deeper state of meditation in the form of a power sound that energizes your intention and unveils your inner potential. It shifts you from mental to supramental and bypasses the neocortex for a quantum leap. Mantras shift you from the cognitive to the heart/consciousness. With mantras you experience a point of singularity which moves you from gross to subtle, and creates a refined point of melding and coherence into the morphogenetic fields. Experience the mantra passively by letting go. You are a spiritual being and able to access the quantum field by mere prompting of your breath. In meditation is where you will heal the core of your being. Once you complete your meditation and chanting of mantras, and you have harnessed tremendous chi (energy) into your body, rub your ears. Let us circulate that energy that has been harnessed through meditation throughout your entire body.

The ears contain acupressure points for every area in your body. Specific parts of the ears correspond to specific parts of the body. Well-trained professionals such as Dr. Terry Oleson, a psychobiologist and Research Director at the American University of Complementary Medicine, Chair of the Department of Psychology at the California Graduate Institute, and faculty at Quantum University, can make very accurate auricular diagnosis with this unconventional clinical procedure of auriculotherapy. Dr. Oleson has published thirty articles and two books on auriculotherapy. Many doctors in various disciplines across the globe have utilized auriculotherapy for managing chronic pain, acute sprains, and reduction of side effects from opioids. The stimulation of the outer ear through acupuncture can affect medical conditions in other parts of the body. The acupressure points in the ear are aligned in the shape of a human body in an inverted position. The head would be at the lobe, and the feet at the top of the ear. Do make use, therefore, of this very convenient organ for your healing.

Holding a crystal, which magnifies consciousness, in your left hand which is connected to your right brain hemisphere, will attune you more quickly to higher dimensions. This part of your cerebral hemisphere has crystalline connections to the third eye pineal gland over the left cerebral hemisphere. You might even place the crystal on a specific chakra which may need special healing and attention. For instance if you are having cardiac issues, place crystals on your heart chakra. The crystals will put out additional positive energies into that chakra. The bigger the disease the more crystals you may need to create a bigger field strength for more measurable therapeutic effects. There is a measurable expression of consciousness within constantly pulsating crystals that will enhance and facilitate your movement upward and forward. Crystals are constantly giving off positive energy, so utilize them to amplify your own healing or someone else's.

My favorite crystal is the amethyst. It radiates pure peace and tranquility. I cherish the purple hues of this quartz which color is intimately connected to cellular replication. Furthermore, the alchemical nature of this color crystal puts out powerful, energizing and purifying properties and opens the third eye. It is also intricately connected with the crown chakra. I have several pieces of amethyst crystals as well as a sizable rock of pink quartz crystal. The amethyst is an ideal crystal to place around the heart chakra since the amethyst is very much associated with the life-force. Since our life-force runs through our bloodstream, it will energize the blood flowing to this organ. Hold it over the heart for approximately ten minutes. It is the crystal of love and extends to all areas of healing. One cannot err with an amethyst in their possession.

Use crystals in your chakra work and in your meditations. Meditation is a time for recalibration and reorientation. Through meditation you will remember your true nature, that of perfection. You were raised to believe you are imperfect and broken. This is an impossibility. These are lies for control that have imprisoned you. Your teachings have made you ordinary when you are extraordinary. Your orthodox teachings have assassinated your soul by keeping you ignorant. Your teachings have made you a beggar when you are a King! Your teachings have kept you small like a grasshopper when you are a Giant and supremely Divine! From the perfect can only come perfection. Going deep into your Silence, you will awaken the Light within you. Breathe inward. You are an extraordinary being!

Quantum meditation will take you into your true and perfect nature as it will help you to look out at life through your own window not someone else's. It will shift you from the world of dualism to a nondualistic reality by giving you a vision of the Self. Meditation will show you how joyous is the inner world over the outer world. Your inner world is extraordinary and full of synchronicities. Quantum meditation will destroy the darkness and open your inner eye. It will unfold your inner grace and show you what an incredible and wonderful creation you are. Hitch a ride. I think you will like the infinite subway.

Edgar Mitchell, the sixth man to walk on the moon, had a noetic transformative experience of this infinite subway when he was returning back to earth from his walk on the moon. He became fully aware that everything and everyone is interconnected and that everyone comes from the same Source. This revelation and awakening happened spontaneously while looking at the Earth from the spacecraft window of his shuttle. He became aware that most people are consumed by greed and ego and are missing the bigger picture. He experienced everything as Oneness in ecstasy. Inspired by this awakening in 1973, he devoted his time, energy, and investments toward research in the areas of consciousness. He also developed the Institute of Noetic Sciences headquartered in California that continues research in spirituality and human potential. Edgar Mitchell has now transitioned but his impact continues to be felt worldwide.

Quantum meditation, which helps you to become receptive to an expanded inner state, is not merely for your spiritual life. It is also for your physical and worldly life. There are many science-based benefits to meditation. Meditation reduces stress, lowers blood pressure, improves attention span, amps up your immune system, controls anxiety and improves emotional health because it brings you peace. Meditation increases calmness so that it helps you to pass exams more easily and helps you cope with illness. It improves your overall health and well-being. It improves relationships. Your strength and courage will grow. It is a wonderful anti-aging activity. You will become radiant. Meditation is transformative which is the reason that few people which cross my path escape my training in meditation.

Quantum meditation quickly shifts you toward coherence in the presence of intention and focus. There is significant research offered by Jon Kabat-Zin, an American Professor Emeritus of medicine and a student of Zen Buddhism, on how meditation helps one to embrace pain and thrive in the face of it. As a daily meditator of almost forty years, I know from direct experience how meditation develops significant body and emotional awareness. I did a root canal and several other medical procedures without anesthetic, under meditation, strictly through transcending the third dimension.

Dharma Singh Kalsa, M.D. and Cameron Stauth in their book, _Meditation as Medicine_ discuss at length the numerous benefits of meditation especially for medical health:

> It creates a unique hypometabolic state in which metabolism is at an even deeper state of rest than during sleep. During sleep oxygen consumption drops by eight percent but during meditation it drops by ten

to twenty percent. Meditation is the only activity that reduces blood lactate, a marker of stress and anxiety. The calming hormones melatonin and serotonin are increased by meditation, and the stress hormone cortisol is decreased by meditation. Meditation has a profound effect on three indicators of aging: Hearing ability, blood pressure and vision of close objects. Long term meditators experience 80 percent less heart disease and 50 percent less cancer than non-meditators. Seventy-five percent of insomniacs were able to sleep normally when they meditated and 34 percent of chronic pain patients significantly reduced medication with meditation.

Quantum meditation grounds you in getting beyond social status, hierarchies and castes because it reminds you of your Oneness. I recall an incident in the mid 1990's when I was invited to speak at the Institute of Neurology in Bangalore. When I returned back to New Delhi, my host and two other men called a taxi and took me out for dinner. The three men exited the taxi and then helped me out. As I walked out of the taxi, I summoned the driver to join us. He did not move, nor respond, and bowed his head. The three men simultaneously and abruptly stopped me in alarm and assured me that cannot happen, that the driver cannot join us in the restaurant. I inquired as to why that was. They mumbled something about the caste system and that the driver joining us in the restaurant "absolutely cannot occur." I then returned back into the taxi joining the driver and politely asked the three men to bring us both dinner in the car! They rubbed their heads in disbelief, spun around for a few seconds on their heels on the road huddled together, and seemingly debated what to do next. I assured them I would not leave the driver in the car alone and unfed while the rest of us communed together while we ate. I softly instructed them, again, to go in and bring our two meals to the car. I dared to challenge the dharma of their caste! They realized I was steadfast in my position. One of them, very reluctantly, went into the restaurant and shortly returned summoning both the driver and me to join them within. The five of us ate together. I engaged the driver in conversation, but the three men did not interact with him as if he had leprosy. I noticed the driver ate quietly, quickly, and with his head down. He was the first to return to the cab. I myself returned to the cab shortly thereafter with the three men behind me. The driver greeted me with a smile of seeming gratitude when I entered the cab.

Quantum meditation propels you into this type of development of your Oneness so you can reach your highest potential. As you slip into meditation you unfold your inner being. A young client just initiating her meditation practice commented she met her soul for the first time. "I found myself falling deeper and deeper into meditation as I focused on my breath. In that moment it was as if I was meeting my Spirt and my soul for the first time. I heard a calm gentle voice saying to me, 'Hi, it's nice to finally talk to you.' And in that moment, I knew I was there to listen and be guided." A physician sitting for his first session of meditation training, wore a huge grin coming out of meditation. When I inquired about the grin, he said embarrassedly, "I had an erection!" Another woman commented that she often has spontaneous orgasms in meditation. Explosions of light in meditation are common especially with experienced meditators but they happen to new initiates as well. I have personally wept and laughed uncontrollably in meditation. Other times, my body began to vibrate at such high speeds, I felt exhausted and "worked over" by end of session. When Spirit enters your body and moves through you, expect the unexpected.

Let your breath be natural and your mind will quiet down. Mind is Consciousness assuming limitations. In meditation you reach a place where limitations, caste and status do not exist because you will learn through meditation that all distinctions are artificial in the Blue Light of meditation. Quantum meditation takes you into the country of Oneness.

Systematically and with persistence, you will go deeper and deeper into your Silence within by gliding through the four bodies of the gross, subtle, causal and Consciousness, the transcendent state. So turn your gaze inward. God is YOU. No one else and nowhere else. There is nothing but you! God is your inner Self. Supreme Silence resides within you. It pulsates at a very deep vibrational level. Once you connect with this silence, you are never alone. Go roam in this silence. Sever your conditioned bondage and live in your new world. Rest here. However, don't be impatient. Nothing of quality happens without effort. You do not become an accomplished violinist overnight. You struggle with finger placement and how to read your music and also struggle with daily practice. You do not become a beautiful ballerina dancer without daily practice. Meditation is not any different. It also takes plenty of daily practice for it to become your art of awakening. You will open yourself up in direct proportion to how dedicated you become to your practice. Liken it to going to the gym. You go once a week or once a month, you will have a good workout, but none of the cumulative physical results for which you might be hoping. You go daily to the gym, you will transform your physical body. If you meditate once a week or once a month, you will have a few minutes of calm and relaxation. If you meditate daily, you will experience first a subtle and then radical transformation from the inside out. Train like an athlete!

Quieting the mind may also be a challenge because the monkey-mind goes from one branch of thought to another. You will constantly have to start over and over. As you persist you will succeed. Even as a seasoned meditator, I can assure you, that it has its seasons even for me. There are times when I can settle in easily and other times things are turbulent. You have to tune your mind like you do a guitar. When it feels tight, loosen it; when it feels loose, tighten it. You have to bring yourself into tune. This way the hustle and bustle of the world will become your meditation and not just in silence. Do not use meditation to escape because you cannot reach your divinity without being in the world and accepting its imperfections. Rather, transform these imperfections through your divinity one breath at a time, and by constantly being aware that your graces do not lie in material achievements or possessions but in your unhorizoned inner peace. To expect this transformation without meditation is like expecting to find water in the Sahara Desert.

I have been meditating for forty years daily. Without this meditation I feel certain I would not, nor could not, have continued to service the world and surrendered myself so humbly to my craft (my clinical practice) for the last forty years. It has created a protective cocoon of energy around me. Therefore, by doing this deep work, meditation has helped me to serve the world authentically. I wake up at 4:30 a.m. to start my meditation. The mind is very fresh, clear, and alert at this time. Meditating first thing in the morning also sets the tone for the rest of the day. The benefits of this early meditation stay with me and aid me in meeting the obstacles of any unforeseeable events. As well, these early morning hours are the times when the endocrine/hormonal system is regulating itself. Therefore, meditation in these early hours assists this process. I started meditating for twenty minutes per day initially and now I meditate for much longer periods. Eventually you will discover that all of life is meditation.

I recommend first thing in the morning before you eat breakfast. If you meditate after a meal, your body is busy digesting, and may not allow you to get relaxed. I recommend early morning because at the same time that meditation relaxes you it is also storing energy which will be available to you for the rest of the day. However, whenever you can carve a time is when it will work for you. Find a time that suits your schedule and temperament. If you find your motivation waning, perhaps join a meditation group and do your practice with like-minded people who understand the value of turning inward. If there isn't a group in your area, start one.

When our children were young, I would meditate around 9:30 in the morning after I helped send them both off to school and cleaned the breakfast table. Now, as our children are adults and in their own homes, I like to awaken at 4:30 a.m. to meditate, and chant and do reiki and long-distance healing toward other loved ones. Those first two hours of the day from 4:30 a.m. to 6:30 a.m. are mine. These are sacred hours for me as I peel the layers of ignorance from my mind. The rest of the day belongs to everybody else.

In quantum meditation the energy of Consciousness is transmitted and you will go beyond gender. You will become pure conscious energy, the all-pervasive Chiti. In meditation I breathe my Master Teacher (Kriya Babaji) into me, and I am then the breath that flows out. We become the breath of one dance. The Guru's name becomes my mantra. I flood my body with my teacher knowing that we become that on which we meditate the most. My spiritual teacher vibrates in my heart; he vibrates in every part of my body. I meditate on his name, knowing his very nature is God also, until he and I become One! Nothing has ever given me such unparalleled joy! I don't need the immortal Babaji, I want him. He is a constant reminder that if he, the deathless immortal Master, at once a mortal, as well succeeded, so will I. Furthermore, the inspiration I receive by conjoining with his consciousness prevents entropy in my own human thoughts and emotions. I feel uplifted by the mere thought of him. His consciousness aids me in staying attuned. Attunement has a decisive influence on our decisions in life. Therefore, I meditate with great love and reverence toward his image and energy. I cannot explain sufficiently nor grasp the magnitude of this experience. Yet the magnanimous energy of Babaji is my next focused stepping-stone in my spiritual evolution. I cannot say his name without bursting into smiles. I want to drown myself in his name Babaji Babaji Babaji. This immortal spiritual giant, Babaji instructed us, "The secret of secrets is that: From Nothingness is the everything created!"

These words of Babaji were demonstrated to me by a brilliant young mathematician in April of 2011 at which point I had written an article for our local newspaper entitled *Nothing is Everything.* In this article I had discussed how the cosmos was created from nothing which reflects how nothing can create a quantum leap. If you were to sum up everything, it would total to zero because everything came from nothing.

It would stand to reason, then, to say that advancement does not come from complicated activities and systems. Simplicity and time can lead to very complex life experiences. Then if you repeat simple operations over and over again, without really needing to know everything when you start, you will emerge with a huge difference and multiple possibilities.

When you simply meditate a little every day and whisper internally "thank you and I love you," you clean off layers of old data that no longer serve you well. The more often you clean the deeper you go into yourself. You will discard so much nonessential data that you will reach your place of nothingness, your zero point – your place of infinite possibilities. By accessing your zero point, a space of infinite power, you will make all your wishes come true on condition that your intentions are pure and are not meant to cause harm. If you remain in this state of mind every day, these Invisible Forces will work in your favor and will smile on you in all areas of your life. Or, perhaps, we don't need to do any of this because there really is no *out there* out there. That perhaps your observations create your universe. So is consciousness perhaps a hoax or an illusion?

It was this one particular article, *"Nothing is Everything"*, of several that I had written for the newspaper, that received the most responses by emails, phone, and regular mailings directly to me. Apparently, its influence continues as one day a young mathematician, Jennifer L., came across this same article. She telephoned me most excitedly saying, "Dr. Daunter, if you will give me only fifteen minutes of your time in your office, I will show you mathematically how true your philosophical position is that '*Nothing is Everything.*' You know it philosophically; I will show you mathematically." Ofcourse, I gladly gave this enthusiastic young mathematician the fifteen minutes she requested.

And show me she did! With large banner paper and pencil in hand, Jennifer confidently demonstrated graphically how as the denominator grows smaller, the numerator increases. This is said very simplistically, as her demonstration was quite complex and elaborate and I could not re-explain it to someone else. Yet, Jennifer continued to display on banner paper, how as we get into negative zero, the numerator increases exponentially. I got it, I really got it!

This is truly God's Math, and exemplifies Babaji's Nothingness as the Source of everything. I could see that there is a positive infinity of numbers as numbers never end and a negative infinity of numbers as there is not a unified sum of all the negative numbers. It all just continues on. Just like life. "So zero," she went on, "represents the everything of math" as of life! That is exactly what Babaji teaches us as the secret of secrets.

Zero is nothing and everything. Zero has a value greater than all numbers. Such as meditation, the simple act of *being* is much more powerful than the act of doing. The simplest act has value over the greatest and most complex behavior.

I realize it takes time and thought to adjust to this paradigm shift, this type of thinking, when we have been conditioned to see life otherwise. Yet, it might be worth reflecting that zero is not nothing but the largest value of both positive and negative. It is an infinite whole containing all numbers – all life! This is God's Math! This is math without time. This is non-linear life, non-spatial and timeless. Simplicity, therefore, is a complete and infinite value. So what we envision as empty in life is really full and infinite.

Math is never finite. Neither are you ever finite. What a radical shift in one's perspective you might say! Yet I have seen how simplicity leads to surprising depth in one's life if one lives with mindfulness and awareness if one walks through life awake rather than sleep walks. Simplify so the unnecessary falls by the wayside and the necessary may speak. Eliminate physical and spiritual clutter, yes spiritual clutter as well. Quit chasing the latest spiritual fad and just SIT...just BE....stillness for healing!!! Sit still to heal your aching soul! The best thing in life is nearest to you – the breath in your nostril. Your breath is always there. Use it and simplify. As Leonardo da Vinci said, "Simplicity is the ultimate sophistication!" Dare you try it – empty abundance or chosen simplicity? Like a sculptor, his beautiful creation is a process of elimination! The essential nature of reality is emptiness! This emptiness, this nothingness, is the source of all life and form.

For those of you who prefer to be guided in meditation, go to the resource page at end of this book. There you will find a twenty-five-minute meditation recording which I taped in a professional studio for you. This recording is suitable to those with no experience with meditation and for advanced meditators as well. A user of the tape left this review of her experience with the meditation: "This is by far one of the most powerful meditations I have ever done. I have experienced an inner state of peace within the first few moments which allowed me to focus and to let go of all the distracting and worrisome thoughts roaming around in my head. What I found so beautiful was the narrator's voice, coming through me. It felt real and genuine so that I could put my trust into it. It definitely was the orchestrations of the narrator's Higher Intelligence that put this masterpiece together. Needless to say, I will be adding this meditation to my daily repertoire of practicing good inner hygiene for the progress of my soul's journey into higher awareness." Perhaps it will be of value to the readers of this book as well.

Being guided in meditation helps you to stay focused and to stay on track. Meditate on your inner Self. Your mind will become that on which you meditate. The more you meditate, the deeper you will go and the greater calmness and peace you will find because you will better understand the origins of your conditioning that have hit you from multiple sources. The more you meditate, the more you will kill the roots of orthodoxy. Once you clear out all these irritants, you will reach the ground of Consciousness. This acute awareness through meditation will prove invaluable as you reach higher and higher forms of understanding. If you can breathe, you can meditate. It is simplicity itself. It changes you one small step at a time. Find out for yourself. One young client who is new to meditation informed me that since she has meditated and done self reiki for the last month, she has found no need for the medical marijuana she had been using and "even my husband noticed I am not smoking and that my energy level is so consistently good." Give it a try and stop living like you are dead in a utilitarian existence where you have given up your needs for that of majority thinking or "normalcy." Drop this unwholesomeness. Find your wholeness inside. Do not practice to find your God. Practice to behave like God since you already are Infinite Intelligence. Gain a deeper sanity.

Once you feel confident with the above style of meditation, then you may want to seek out Babaji's Kriya Yoga. This form of meditation, of which it has many imposters, frees your soul consciousness to make extremely rapid progress toward your evolution and self-realization. It is a lightning path to your personal growth. Forty-four second cycle of Babaji's Kriya breath gives you one year of natural spiritual unfoldment we have been informed by Paramahansa Yogananda and other devotees of Babaji.

In Kriya Yoga, or Yoni Mudra, you block your ears, eyes and nasal passage with your thumbs, index and middle fingers. These positions will provide you the experience of both Light and Sound. Light and Sound nourish in different ways, yet awaken you in the same direction to One Source. It is through the sound of drumming by a Native American at a conference that I initially began experiencing the colors of the chakras. Light illuminates and sound self-realizes. Through Kriya Yoga, the tip of your tongue should touch the palate just behind the upper teeth. This tongue position will eliminate the accumulation of saliva and eliminate the need to swallow. It will also maintain the flow of circular energy without a break. Then you withdraw and concentrate on ajna, your third eye, your seat of Consciousness. As you are practicing Kriya, you breathe energy up from your root chakra to the crown chakra and then breathe back down from the crown to the front of your face and breathe down the front of your body to the root chakra. You keep the breath moving in this circular motion to imitate the kundalini energy which will naturally release as you continue to meditate. You keep your life force moving up and down through your sushumna, where your life force is concentrated, to awaken your sleeping kundalini and life force. Your inner body is a fortress of 72,000 nadis of which one is most important, sushumna, and seven major chakras. Sushumna runs from the top chakra in the crown, sahasrara, where Consciousness resides, to your tailbone chakra, muladara, where Kundalini rests. Kundalini means your total potential. It is a focused energy that lies coiled like a serpent in muladhara chakra awaiting to be awakened. You can keep this kundalini in seed form in Consciousness or you can manifest it into the physical consciously. Awakening this kundalini through meditation is a way of manifesting your potential. Kundalini, and all activities in your life, run through your sushumna. As the kundalini rises through the sushumna, you begin to activate each of the individual chakras.

This Kriya meditation is so powerful, that a few breaths, perhaps three, is all a novice might consider doing initially. Then gradually increase as energy and experience dictates. I was instructed to only do three breaths as well when I was initiated in Kriya. When I went home, I thought if three is good, twenty will be better. That evening I purged orally and rectally and through my dreams. My dream was most interesting and symbolic as I saw many black carcasses on the floor of my bedroom and three very large white swans! I translated this dream as significant karmas having been burnt off (black carcasses) with graces emerging and rising to the surface (white swans) at different evolutionary stages. The three swans on the front cover of this book represent this dream: Consciousness, the subtle and the gross......the triune. Swans, the largest of the waterfowl, embody to this author eternal life with their white color symbolic of their purity and light. Swans are known for harnessing physics to take off into the air at different stages rendering them masters of the sky! We, as well, need to harness physics to make ourselves masters of the Ocean.

More graces flowed through me as a result of meditation. I never had training in art, nor did I ever aspire to become an artist, although I have always very much enjoyed trips to art museums. Then art literally began erupting through me one day and I couldn't not paint. I had an inner prompting to go purchase paint and was inspirationally led toward watercolor, for a reason unknown to me at that moment, as I knew nothing about painting mediums. I now love the way watercolor dances on paper and lets through light. It is such a spiritual medium and meets my soul's needs. Within months of this inner explosion in art, someone "discovered" my work, and asked me to do a solo exhibit. This was the first solo exhibit in this art center as typically they combined several artists together in the studio for their exhibits. I painted forty-seven paintings in a seven-month period and sold seventy paintings in a three-year period! This inspiration erupted through meditation and was another grace bestowed upon me. I was/am in as much awe as you may be in reading about this gifted experience. I cannot replicate the original art no matter how hard I may try. Because I do not believe my art has anything to do with me, but is Spirit's work, I donate every cent from my art to charities.

Creating these paintings was like being a visual musician. It was all a part of the music of Spirit. I would sit in front of my watercolor paper, meditate for as long as needed, until I received inspiration. I knew nothing about color theory. I had no desire, nor have any desire, to produce art that is merely decorative of big vista scenes of which I could simply take a photograph. I so appreciate this type art, and all art, because they require enormous skill; however, personally, I want and need to paint with my soul, from within, through my inner eyes, and not through my physical eyes. I want to focus on abstract spiritual art inspired by my inner voice and inspired by my soul. I want my art to be simple, uncluttered in detail and a sacred portal into Consciousness so the viewer will make not only a physiological but a spiritual connection to the art. I value what Leonardo da Vinci, an Italian genius painter of the High Renaissance, had to say about art and life:

> Simplicity is the ultimate sophistication.
> When once you have tasted flight, you will forever walk the earth with your eyes turned skyward, for there you have been, and there you will always long to return.
> Learning never exhausts the mind.
> Art is never finished, only abandoned.
> Painting is poetry that is seen rather than felt, and poetry is painting that is felt rather than seen.
> The human foot is a masterpiece of engineering and a work of art.

It had long since come to my attention that people of
accomplishment rarely sat back and let things happen
to them. They went out and happened to things.
I have been impressed with the urgency of doing.
Knowing is not enough; we must apply. Being willing
is not enough; we must do.
As a well-spent day brings happy sleep, so a life well
spent brings happy death.
Water is the driving force of all nature.

I share with you now a beautiful verse my soul composed during
a period in quantum meditation. I recite it as often as possible before
I enter meditation or before I retire in the evening. It dissolves me
in praise of the Great Source. I send it to all the readers as a gift from
my heart to yours.

RAISING THE HEART

Oh Spirit, who is imminent in all things,
Omniscient and all knowing
I bow to Thee.
I enter into silence and unite with Thy Divine Will.
I surrender to That within me.
You are Consciousness. You are Unbounded.
Oh spirit, sustain me spiritually and physically
By blessing me with your inflowing Grace.
Fill me with love and charity.
And erase from me the cloud of unknowing
In order that I may become more in tune
To my own Divinity and the Divinity in all.
Take me from the night to the Light.
Continue to infuse me with Thy Grace
And the patience and perseverance
Essential for spiritual success.

Do not assume that because you meditate you will not feel anger or jealousy or resentment. What you will do, however, is not judge your feelings or evaluate them. Rather, you will recognize them and not suppress them. Such emotions are not incompatible with you as a meditator nor with your spiritual life. They are part of being human. You do not stop being human because you meditate. You stop being judgmental and you become aware and awake. Open yourself up to your emotions and do not struggle against them. Emotions are transient. They come and they go. Quantum meditation will cause you to feel sensitive to the emotional attunement of others as well. This is a pre-warning so tune in to it to safeguard your own emotional attunement by protecting your sacred space.

Also, do not assume that because you meditate you will escape illnesses. St. Teresa of Avila is a perfect example of this. She was saintly, vocal, an activist, and a visionary and suffered with severe ailments all her life despite all the meditations and prayers. Source knows that we can be fainthearted, so we will be given trials against our will so we can come out stronger at the end. Infinite Consciousness has many ways of awakening our soul. Rest assured you will have many occasions from which to profit. So do not think everything is lost. Experience will show you the tremendous gains that come through such paths. You will also have some dark nights. Such trials will make your soul fly even higher because some illnesses will reach to your soul's depths in ways unimaginable. Source has the power to do things that your intellect will not understand. Humility, therefore, is at the foundation of all your progressive evolution.

QUANTUM MEDICINE,
MEDICINE OF THE INFINITE

An invasion of armies can be stopped,
but not an idea whose time has come.
Victor Hugo

Quantum medicine is emerging an exciting new vision of medical care that uses the principles of quantum physics. Quantum medicine is the medicine of the Infinite and a necessary component of quantum spirituality. Its foundation is non–locality, quantum entanglement and discontinuous quantum leaps in Consciousness to understand the individual in all his layers for proper medical intervention. It depathologizes disease in a human being and looks into your inner core (potentia). This will have far reaching implications for you as an individual and on the collective

Quantum medicine has quickly seen the flaws of Newtonian physics which informs allopathic conventional medicine. The latter model creates a very limited view of you and does not consider your potential beyond your physical body. Furthermore, there is tremendous wastage and prostitution in the capitalist medical system. You are not a mere biological computer controlled by your brain and your peripheral nervous system. Healing is not merely physiological. Your body is in a dynamic interplay with subtle vital energy fields that require rebalancing if any healing is to take place. The chakras, your spiritual spine, must be considered in this vital subtle system since we know that they are the body of your soul. By rebalancing your subtle energy system, which is where your health and vitality are decided, you rebalance your cellular system. All disease starts at the subtle level as well. This rebalancing and clearing can be done for example through the acupuncture meridian system which has become more accepted by conventional medicine in the last few years especially for pain. Acupuncture can revitalize your subtle body which then revitalizes your physical body. The meridians are the interface between the physical body and the subtle body. This is where healing must start. Conventional medicine is the master in replacing diseased organs; yet has limited knowledge in how to prevent diseases as of yet because they have no conception of your animated life-force and subtle energy fields. This is where healing must start because it is at this level that diseases originate.

The new physician requires specialized training to realize that matter is energy and that matter is frozen light; that beneath the electrophysiological and hormonal function is a dynamic and subtle energetic system which coordinates all activity. It is these subtle energetic systems that influence all your cellular patterns. However, allopathic medicine does not yet have sufficient technology to access the subtle fields. Quantum medicine does utilize ample technology to analyze the changes that are taking place in your subtle energetic fields and treat the abnormal etheric patterns before they manifest into the physical. We know that measurable changes in the subtle body precede the pathology that we see in the physical body. This allows quantum medical physicians to do early detection rather than management by crisis.

The outdated conventional model needs to be updated to include these higher energy systems which are very fluid unlike the dense physical system. The merging of the two systems, conventional and quantum, would allow one to seek quantum medical amelioration with augmentation from western medical sources when necessary. This merger might be stirring through Integrative Medicine, a branch that combines both alternative and conventional treatments. A marriage of quantum and allopathic medicine is the ideal rather than one over the other. The Buddha instructed, "*If you hold a string too tight, it will snap. If you hold a string too loose, it won't play.*" The path to enlightenment is between two extremes. It is about finding a middle way as the Buddha often instructed. It is about finding a middle way as well in medicine and health.

Much of society is exhausted with measured doses of drugs to influence their physical bodies for mere temporary relief. The body needs to be able to have time to self-heal through its own energetic feedback loop which can repair and regenerate a broken-down body. Western physicians need to support their patients in this process or patients need to say to their physician exactly what one of my cancer patients said to her oncologist when she wanted to explore promising natural treatments, "If you do not support me, I will go to the doc next door who will!"

Even in our brokenness we need to see the divine in our patients and we need to mirror this divinity. Even in our brokenness we need to continue to live. In our brokenness we realize that healing comes in many forms. A young, 32-years of age, mature beautiful sensitive friend of mine whose husband recently transitioned from a glioblastoma multiform stage IV, an inoperable brain tumor, said to me that allopathic physicians exhausted them at the end of her husband's life because of their limited view of the human being. So much so that she and her husband broke off contact with them toward the end of his life. She further commented, "You have to be alive even while you are dying!" What profound words coming from someone so young. Despite that allopathic physicians stripped them of all hope, this highly spiritually evolved couple knew that there is more to them than just the survival of the limiting factors of the physical brain and body, and she and her husband continued to nourish the subtle spiritual to the very end because they knew the spirit body never dies. Her husband transitioned at the highest vibration of himself. They understood very clearly that all perceived reality is a fiction. We are not a closed system but one that is in dynamic flow and equilibrium.

It must be understood that through your subtle vital dynamic energetic system of different frequencies, you are able to access higher and deeper states of consciousness. Your physical body cannot exist without your subtle bodies. Thus, you can be taught to access such higher levels of information for your healing. Without this spiritual dimension, conventional medicine, which has become politicized, has grave consequences and will never accomplish healing. Furthermore,

135

often life-saving medical treatment is censored for profit, and what is prescribed has nothing to do with the correct understanding of the science. Conventional medicine will merely continue to treat symptoms based on profit as they have been doing for decades. Unfortunately, the hands of many sincere allopathic medical professionals are tied behind their backs by their governments who are bedmates with pharmaceutical companies. Pharmacokinetic and surgical procedures are crude approaches and need to be updated by information available through quantum physics. Furthermore, pharmacological treatment is often determined by how well they line the pockets of the pharmaceutical companies rather than by least harm and greater effectiveness. We need to disconnect from our pharmaceutical system. Quantum medicine sees you as a multidimensional being with different levels of frequency and treats the whole person from the inside out not the outside in. Consciousness is behind all the cellular expression which affects our physical body. Consciousness = All. This is the equation of infinity.

There is tremendous utility in using subtle realms for healing in clinical and medical practices. We do not need to understand it to see it work. I treated a young couple with unexplained infertility. The woman, Lisa, had gone through years of fertility treatments and several other engineered maneuvers to attempt to get pregnant. All these unsuccessful attempts caused even further stress. Her intense craving for a child was causing hyper-anxiety. There is significant physical and emotional strain associated with attempted parenthood especially when someone places high value on starting a family. Knowing that conception is more than a biological event at a molecular level, and that the psyche and spirit play a major role, I suggested she allow me to train her in meditation. We do not treat with meditation; we treat in meditation. The meditation was directed towards stress reduction, ego strengthening and normalizing biological barriers. I suggested she meditate twice a day for at least twenty-minutes. I also suggested to Lisa that she do a pelvic roll, to release blocked energy, as if she was playing with a hula hoop, twenty in each direction, at least three times a day. Lisa became pregnant within two months and gave birth to a healthy male child.

In another case of infertility, Janice, a premenopausal woman had been told for years she was infertile. Consequently, she never practiced birth control. She suddenly found herself pregnant at a very inopportune time in her life. This pregnancy began creating significant imbalance in her marriage and overall family life. Abortion or adoption were not options for Janice. I trained Janice in meditation. Instructed her that if she spoke with sincere fervor and authenticity of spirit to her unborn child, and informed the child that this was very poor timing and that she could not love it in the way it deserved to be loved, then the unborn child will relinquish its spirit from her body and remove itself from her womb within 72 hours. A week later, Janice went to her gynecologist for a second ultrasound. The gynecologist could still see the embryonic sac but no embryo was visible and no signs of miscarriage were noted by her physician. Her gynecologist was dumb-founded Janice told me and the doctor remarked as she shrugged her shoulders, "I don't know what happened and I don't understand it." To which Janice responded, "But *I* do!"

We are electromagnetic beings. Our experiences, desires and thoughts know no bounds. Furthermore, these cases are examples that there are invisible realms which we can access for our healing. Healing, therefore, is a creative act requiring a movement up into the invisible subtle realities.

The most dramatic case I treated in an altered state of consciousness was the case of Larry, a very bright 35-year-old American professional who had developed a severe sexual obsession. He informed me that he had been in therapy for ten years unsuccessfully. His sexual obsession dominated his life and disrupted his marriage. He was fixated on women's breasts and fell into a trance gazing at breasts even in the company of his wife. He was fully aware how hurtful this behavior was to his wife. He felt no control over his obsession and commensurate behavior. He became alarmed when this obsession began to generalize toward his female children. Larry's wife attested to the sincerity and authenticity of her husband and that he was exemplary in other areas of his life.

Larry was a highly moral and ethical man. This behavior frightened him and he became severely clinically depressed. He felt great shame and guilt and became suicidal. Because of his suicidal ideations, pharmacological treatment was initiated. The medications helped his depression, but not his obsession which seemed to have a life of its own. The sexual obsession rendered him unable to hold a full-time job for any length of time. He held meager jobs way below his potential despite his extensive training in his career field.

I waited for full stabilization of his depression before introducing a light trance state. In this trance, Larry entered a state beyond his usual boundaries. Larry entered a past life when at age four he had been placed in an orphanage under the care of a husband and wife. There were fifteen other boys in this orphanage. He quickly became the mistress's favorite child. She took him with her often for recreation. By age twelve, she started inviting him for dinner alone and eventually began taking him into her bedroom. One day she undressed in front of Larry and reached down for his hand to explore and manipulate her very large breasts. Eventually she required him to suckle her breasts as she fondled his head for long periods of time between her breasts. This became a nightly ritual. He described these moments in great detail amidst torrential tears. Larry was hopelessly and helplessly over–stimulated, sobbed himself to sleep, and was significantly fearful of the consequences if he refused her demands. He felt trapped. He was tormented by this emotional and sexual prison at age twelve. He often contemplated suicide because of his circumstances.

Larry's ability to recollect this past life experience provided a catalyst for resolving his present life circumstances. He understood his present life obsessions from a more expanded perspective which helped him achieve emotional integration. His shame melted away into understanding and self-acceptance. His sexual obsession remitted. Last contact I had with Larry he had held down a job in his career field for a solid four years with no further resurgence of symptoms of the sexual obsession. He was off all medications. His energy and interests seemed boundless.

In accessing a subtle realm of consciousness, Larry fanned his burning flame and brought it to the surface. Significant emotional participation occurred when his deeply hidden material was released. With skillful techniques, the meaningfulness of the data was integrated into full awareness. In recalling this past life, Larry discharged the energy that was tied up with deep rooted memories so that they no longer created disease.

Although I personally believe in past lives because it offers a logical and intelligent explanation for life in this world for me, I am neutral in therapy about how one interprets these images which come up in trance states. One can view them as past lives, ancestral memories, collective spirit, or merely consciousness's way of transmitting information for greater insight. It is the choice of the patient. I believe that trying to find out merely "who was I in my past lives" is shallow investigation. These regressions need to be about helping us remember the larger cycle of life while they provide us an experience rather than an explanation.

Higher states of consciousness must be recognized and understood as the repertoire of human potential if we are going to move forward, and we have seen significant movement in recent years. Some of this debt is owed to C. G. Jung, for instance, who discovered that the dance of Consciousness influences both dimensions reciprocally, similar to quantum entanglement so that it becomes hard to distinguish one from the other. Therefore, we know we are not biological computers but have transcendent abilities far beyond linear causality. Transcendent experiences strongly influence our health and our spiritual evolution. If you want to heal, you must become more aware of this dimension and cultivate it, because you can no longer hope to heal yourself merely through conventional medicine. The latter functions on an incomplete model. Therefore, it makes incomplete or erroneous diagnoses and incomplete and often ineffective, and, at times life-threatening interventions. The Quantum medicine model is critical not just for you but also for our planet. In the words of Rumi, "Don't go back to sleep."

Western medicine, on its own, *is* a conceptual straightjacket agreed a physician client and often "ineffective, unproductive and dangerous," he further acknowledged. On the other hand, quantum medicine is in alignment with the findings on consciousness research of C. G. Jung and the multidimensional individual. Quantum medicine is inclusive of allopathic medicine, but it does not stop there. It gives an expanded view of you as an individual and of disease by looking into transpersonal dimensions that go far beyond the limits of your human body. Many perennial philosophies implemented in quantum medicine are proving invaluable in health and in healing. Quantum medicine has quanta resources beyond pharmaceuticals and surgery. Therefore, western medicine may want to revise its judgment on these perennial wisdoms and utilize them in its treatment of patients by seeing patients as infinite rather than finite.

Conventional allopathic medicine has failed many people. It has its niche in single system problems requiring surgery, but when an imbalance is multi-dimensional as most illnesses are, it fails more frequently than not. However, in surgical needs, there is no better medical system than the allopathic system. It has also at times, however, become life-threatening or taken life, as it did with my sister, Maria.

My sister, Maria, was killed by the drug prolia, a six-month injection given to her for osteoporosis. Note that once a drug is injected into your body, it cannot be removed. You cannot stop taking it like you do a pill. Maria had an extremely negative reaction to this shot and the way her allopathic team dealt with it was with opioids. So rather than calm positiveness and serene acceptance at the time of her transition, Maria clung to life for as long as she could under the influence of narcotics and life sustaining instruments which trapped her inert and useless body.

Maria was rushed into the Emergency Room (ER) at a hospital near her home three times in a two-week period after having been administered prolia. Three times in a two-week period she was discharged without a diagnosis despite symptoms, i.e. headaches, weakness, and fatigue temporally associated with the administration of the shot prolia. After two weeks on the drug prolia, Maria's heart and lungs collapsed according to her surgeon and was visibly rendered a quadriplegic. It was then and only then that Maria was admitted to the Intensive Care Unit (ICU) where she never left ICU alive. In just ten weeks Maria died of iatrogenic causes, an illness caused by modern medicines. Iatrogenic illness is the third most fatal disease in our country taking the lives of over a quarter million people per year. It is widespread and it should concern you, not just for yourself but for your loved ones.

Maria died screaming from her unbearable pain from a spinal abscess, congestive heart failure, double pneumonia and a quadriplegic body. She became unresponsive and septic. She died on a ventilator with a body so full of edema she was no longer recognizable.

What animated my sister, Maria, as I knew her was no longer in force. The Maria I knew was gone! The butterfly had flown. Was I just mourning for a cocoon? They silenced her screams of anguish with morphine, an opioid. What was left now that her fragile body was silenced? Perhaps she beat them at the illusion of their own game by realizing her true nature. Allopathic medicine imprisoned her, and she broke the trap and expanded into unknown territory.

I wondered if Maria was independent of all this chaotic intervention into her physical body or did the end-of-life narcotics given to Maria result in the oscillation of inhibiting negative energy sine waves which interfered with her smooth transition by diminishing her consciousness at the end-of-life. Opioids, one would think, would interfere with the mind's ability to give form to potentia. We must cast a finer net to not let consciousness slip through.

Having been by Maria's bedside before her final days of transition, it seemed that prolia, which rendered her body quadriplegic and unresponsive from the neck down, and the polypharmacy of opioids which were administered to her by her allopathic team of physicians to manage both her physical and psychological pain caused by the prolia injection, created such an unbearable vortex of isolation and aloneness rather than death being a central aspect of her self-renewal. It is appalling that you can become a victim of not only disease in today's world but also of its treatment. So be most attentive what you allow to be given to you to put in your body. Even more never allow anyone to violate your bodily autonomy by coercion. The karmic propensities of such a cultural medical model, the causal factors of such immoral conduct, cannot even be fathomed.

Maria was far from ready to transition. "I never imagined finding myself in this position. I don't want to die! I want to go back to my flower garden," she pleaded with me as my tears washed her paralyzed legs as I attempted to massage and reiki away death. I never felt so powerless. Feelings of injustice and sadness versus my responsibility to just be with her and get myself out of the way ravaged my soul. Her fear of perishability at an untimely cycle in her vigorous vibrant life may not have allowed her to respond to the rapid metamorphosis which should have been a regenerative evolutionary process.

One may question whether Maria herself deemed that her life had been fulfilled and used this way of transition as the portal away from this existence. Was she the planner within the plan? I kept reminding myself that life is not ruined by death if we value every precious moment we are alive.

The adversities of life were unbearable especially since I knew there were quantum resources that could have helped Maria early on in her pain that would have enhanced her health. At the same time life confronted me with the mysteries of our own existence. I struggled to reconcile that filth is pure in the essential oneness of our being since Consciousness resides in everything. And if Spirit is Infinite, then there cannot be a place that Spirit is not. At the same time, I wanted to dissolve the filth that occupies our lives. I felt hanging at the shadow's edge.

Quantum medicine provides you quantum choices besides polypharmacy or surgery. Furthermore, you have the option to direct your physician to not administer opioids to you at any time and especially at end of life. However, you must give this directive in writing and make sure it is placed in your medical records file with a copy to yourself.

There is a desperate seismic need for a shift in medical care and quantum medicine is the answer. Health care demands a cultural change and teamwork if we are going to be successful in even reducing the $600 billion of unnecessary medical costs that stress not only the patients but our society, because patients experience medical complications from procedures and medical care they do not need. A neuropsychologist friend and colleague was informing me recently over lunch that he burst out to his Oncologist, "You are still at the rat stage in the science of your medical approach!" Rachel Naomi Remen, M.D. was not "modest in speaking truth" when she commented in her extraordinary book Kitchen Table Wisdom, "A medical training is like a disease. It would be years before I would recover from mine!" Advocate for your care and if the doctor treating you is uncooperative than go to the doctor next door who will team up with you in your health care because in order to heal any body they need to know the body electric first.

Quantum medicine, an energy, spiritual, psychoendoneuroimmunologic approach to health, focuses on you as a whole person, empowers and optimizes you by focusing on your well-being rather than on disease. It is a quantum interdisciplinary method that looks at the interactions amongst all factors of your well-being and more specifically the effect of the mind on health and resistance to disease. Even the world-renowned Mayo Clinic has integrated such an approach to health care and has dedicated an entire wing to integrative treatments because over thirty percent of the population prefer and choose something other than allopathic medicine. Mayo Clinic also makes available reiki, a hands-on-healing technology, for pain patients in hemodialysis as a part of its psychoendoneuroimmunologic approach to patient care. Know that you have choices. When these choices are not being provided to you, it is because of ignorance.

Quantum medicine is precision care. It is medicine with soul because it sees you as a finite-infinite expression. Your care is personalized in quantum medicine and there is no such thing as one-size-fits-all. Its focus for you is multi-dimensional and on the root cause rather than just a focus on symptoms. Health care professionals using quantum medicine have complete sets of possibilities and technologies from which to choose for virtually anything to occur for your healing not just drugs and surgery.

It has been determined through physics that energy and information make up this world and every organism that exists on it. Quantum medicine is based on the findings of physics. Being healthy is not a mere absence of symptoms but a process of sufficient energy and proper information from the cellular level. In order to heal anyone, cells need to be freed from their encumbrances. Meditation, qigong, tai chi are methods for circulating natural healing resources especially in cardiovascular, muscular and immunological health. Rather than opioids, acupuncture, paired with infra-red light and stem cell stimulators, has shown remarkable benefits for pain patients. Pulsed Electromagnetic Frequency (PEMF) has plenty of research behind it in its ability to effect changes in pain patients. I have this technology in our own home and it is like having a quantum doctor available daily to me and my family. Not a day goes by that I do not utilize PEMF because it regenerates and restores cellular health. I completed a pilot study on PEMF as a safe, non-invasive, non-addictive alternative to opioids without side effects and the conclusion supported my hypothesis that PEMF would reduce and/or eliminate the use of opioids. The opioid epidemic is of national concern and the problem itself is a practical not a conceptual issue. We all need to care because its tangible effect is innumerable undesirable costs, pain and even death. The pilot study results showed how a quantum medicine approach through PEMF technology improved safety, reduced and/or eliminated participants' need for opioids and improved their overall quality of life.

PEMF housecleans the cells through energy waves that heal the body and improves natural cellular communication that take place at even low intensity levels. It builds magnetic fields which are influenced by electric current around the body that goes deep inside and that are earth compatible. This technology passes completely through the body whether the intensity is high or low. The difference would be the amount of charge the field stimulates in tissues as it passes through the body. Were we all already able to access this energy from Consciousness, one would not need aids, since one would know the body is most capable of healing itself. But since global evolution has not reached that point, proper external supports are needed at times to provide the necessary building blocks and energy for our health and healing. One of those supports is Pulsed Electromagnetic Frequency.

PEMF is a forty-year technology that has been approved by the Federal Drug Administration for pain and non-union fractures and was initially used with astronauts after our first space program. NASA found significant osteoporotic changes as well as severe depression in their astronauts after their return from space trips. Since they have incorporated PEMF, these conditions have been reduced dramatically because it discovered that PEMF maximizes the action potential of every cell by increasing cell permeability. PEMF heals. PEMF regenerates. There are 10,000 plus studies on PEMF and 2000 plus double-blind studies on the efficacy of PEMF. Therefore, there is no reason why every allopathic physician is not well informed on this technology and using it daily in their practice. True that it is not a part of medical training at this point, but it is a part of our scientific research data base. So education and a quick acquisition of information can be had by a quick click on the computer. Dr. Lisa Fortin, M.D., a Michigan-based Regenerative Medicine Specialist, and former Chief of Radiology, has stated that "the benefits of PEMF are so immense and so far-reaching because it reduces pain at the cellular level."

Quantum medicine has Ayurveda to draw on as well, an ancient medicine model that comes to us from India and is 5000 years old and the oldest medical system in continuous practice. Ayurveda has its origins in the rejuvenation and purification of the body in order to assist us toward enlightenment. It prevents disease rather than treats disease. Quantum medicine also utilizes such technologies as the

145

SCIO (Scientific Consciousness Interface Operation System) which is non-invasive and has proven to be an exceptional pre-diagnostic tool for detecting stress before it might even be detectable by a person's consciousness. It is a universal electrophysiological biofeedback system which gathers bioenergetic information regarding a client's mental, physical, emotional and spiritual systems. It is a very sensitive technology, and it is effective with high levels of accuracy. It is an exceptional state of the art technology for stress detection and stress reduction and blends quantum physics, homeopathy, electro-acupuncture and Rife frequencies.

The EDA (Electrodermal Assessment) is another technology which has proven to be very accurate for non-intrusive whole person assessments. EDA measures disturbances in the energetic meridian systems and the organs associated with those systems similar to those utilized in acupuncture and homeopathy. EDA measures functional imbalances in the body through bioenergetic feedback. It is an indispensable technology because it can even determine the dosages of supplements one may need to administer for healing. This is a fifty-year old technology which picks up energetic imbalances and deficiencies that would not be picked up by the allopathic model and would then emerge structurally some years later accompanied with acute or chronic pain. Quantum medicine focuses on prevention rather than management by crisis.

Quantum medicine, is a method of neurophysiology, psychology, and philosophy with a broad spectrum of multi-disciplines to address the complexities of any healing situation. It is an advanced informational medicine that is forever taking you inward to assist you in healing your energy fields from a deep unmanifested level of consciousness. It is absolutely, indisputably a preventative method of healing.

All healing is self-healing. Quantum medicine alerts you to an infinite pool of possibilities for your healing based on the downward causation model. It deepens your relationship with the Divine within you because it nudges you to look at your true and fullest nature for your healing. It provides you numerous ways to find joy and bliss while conventional concepts of medical treatment negate your luminosity. Conventional treatment cannot heal when it negates the most essential part of you.

Health issues at times are challenging and challenges help develop brain plasticity. Through any challenge, focus on love because without love you are stuck in quicksand. Love is the source of your Consciousness and penetrates interdimensionally. Love is an interdimensional lubricant. It is the root of your creative spirit which relates to your Unbounded Spirit and lives in a timeless realm. Every act of love will release blocked energy in the atoms of your body. Love is the absence of fear! As long as fear exists, love cannot. It is your ultimate healer. "Love is the undisturbed balance that keeps this universe together," instructs Babaji.

Seek out a quantum professional for your care who honors Spirit, understands energy as well as your spiritual foundation, and implements quantum techniques that address you as a whole being. Quantum medicine will help you shift from external authority to trust in inner knowing. It will support you and teach you to become a partner in your own healing. It will help you shift from the opium of allopathic and western dogma. Quantum medicine makes it clear that there is something bigger and greater within you that remains untapped which you can access for your healing. There is a central phenomenology in self-healing in which "absolute" knowledge is available in transpersonal fields and from which everything else arises. The inward focus to access these transpersonal fields is the single-mindedness necessary for the process of healing. Quantum medicine uncovers your native organic state of being.

Quantum professionals are Knights of Light relating to your soul as an important component of your healing and transformation. They see you as a continuity in change and a movement in consciousness rather than a bundle of cells, tissues and cartilages and organs. Quantum professionals have broken away from orthodoxy and conditioning. These Knights are helping reshuffle the stardust! These Knights are proving there is a better way to heal and live.

Quantum medicine knows that everything that you need for

a wholesome existence is available to you in your Consciousness which is a perfect equilibrium of pure life force and energy. They help you in accessing this inner medicine in multiple ways. They empower you by consistently reminding you that you have within you all that you need for your healing because Consciousness is the ground of ALL. There is nothing but Consciousness. As your parent atom, Consciousness contains the needed characteristic to produce itself. The atom receives its generative power from Infinite Intelligence. Therefore, you, as well, receive your power from this abstract intelligence of the fifth dimension which continues to infinitely expand into greater dimensional factors. Infinite Creative Intelligence expands in perpetuity to maintain its infinity. Through the evolutionary cycles, consciousness develops into infinite properties again from which you originally descended. It is omnipresent, in everything; it is omnipotent, no greater force exists beyond it. Life is the movement of this energy in perpetuity, and you are collated from this energy. There is no movement of life that exists without its ancillary relationship to this Infinite Intelligence.

Healing, therefore, is clearly scientific because it is a change in energy, a change that only you can create within yourself. The practitioner, a healing polarity, can facilitate this change in a patient, but cannot create it. So do not give your power away to anyone. All is within you. Through the process of quantum entanglement an intention on the part of the practitioner and you will alter your enzymes and hemoglobin values. Hope on the part of your practitioner will have biological implications for you. This has been clearly viewed in blood samples via microscopy.

DOWNWARD CAUSATION MODEL

The Quantum Life is grounded in the downward causation model of quantum spirituality and quantum medicine. The whole acts on all the different parts through a level-entanglement process where the whole has an effect over all the lower levels. This process is only possible through the interconnections of protons, electrons, and neutrons, the wiring of Consciousness. This is where Consciousness (the hardware) takes a complex task and simplifies it by splitting it up into smaller modules of supramental, mental and vital (the software), or sub tasks, and feeds it on to the next higher level where the work is invisible until it gets to its base level, the physical (the computer monitor), where the majority of the visible work is done. It is a rapid dynamic wireless communication system whose direction is guided by meaning and determines its dance. The electron is guided by meaning on its trajectory to accomplish its end. All the levels have to adapt through the process but this adaptation can be changed based on new information which may be provided by the Central Regulator. The levels adapt to the ongoing changes. That is why there is a hierarchal structured symbiosis between your hardware and the software, a relationship of reciprocal influence (quantum entanglement), which give your system purpose and meaning derived from the highest level, Consciousness. The lower levels are doing the work but they are being influenced by the higher levels so they can fulfill higher level purposes. Jesus spoke in the metaphor of this connection when he instructed, "The Father and I are one. Of myself I do nothing, but the Father within does all things."

Quantum uncertainty through quantum effects and indeterminism provide some freedom and slack for the higher levels to operate to the point of potentially changing genetic inheritance of a person for their healing. This effect/response is explained more in depth by Dr. Bruce Lipton in his book <u>The Biology of Belief</u>:

> The fate of the cell is controlled by the conditions of the environment. The blood composition is really the factor that controls the genetic response of the cell. So then, what controls the composition of the culture medium? The blood. The brain is the chemist. The chemistry put into the blood by the brain is a direct complement to the picture we hold in our mind. In other words, the mind's image is translated by the brain into chemistry, which then goes to the body to create a physical complement to the image in the mind. In ancient terms, back from the days of the Buddha, 2500 years ago, 'What we believe, we become.' Basically, our perception changes the chemistry of our blood. Rather than genetic determinism, we can see that genetics can provide a host of possibilities based on the environment (thoughts) with which we surround our cells. One's mental attitude can upregulate or downregulate gene expression to effect health. Genes do not mechanically control one's life, he instructs, thoughts do. This is the study of epigenetics which gives the ability to change conditions with which one may have been born. Epigenetics gives self-empowerment rather than a parasitic attitude that demands that one ideology must be the ideology of all.

Therefore, the thoughts that come from your higher levels (Consciousness, supramental, mental) affect your base levels (vital, physical). I know that your senses and thoughts and undisciplined mind want to deny you that which you already are. You wrestle with accepting that which you can even become. Be attentive because the concept of yourself will alter your future. Think for yourself. Know for certain that Consciousness is all there is. Become fully conscious that you are now that which you no longer wish to be and get out of the desert. Say goodbye to the old self. Let it die off and get used to the new vibration you are coming into. Birth your new self by changing the concept of yourself. There is no one to change but yourself. Whatever you become will shape all the circumstances of your life. There are no further props to lean on any longer. I have told you the Truth. There is no power outside of *you*. You are everything and you are nothing. You are literally existing in the expression of life unfolding. Plant the seed: I AM. Concentrate on that which you already are: I AM. It contains all the power for self-expression. Your dimensionally larger Self will determine how to assist you in uncovering the layers until you access your I AM. Burst with the joy of your discovery and close your ears to anything that may deny your end goal. Live from the top down. Think fourth dimensionally and walk in your new assumption. There is a better way to live.

Beware of the psychotic interpretations of life which so many individuals impose as the dominant interpretation of life upon all. Rather, walk through the doorway of your own integrity to support your evolution. Culture's hypnotic dogma renders you into a trance and is one of disempowerment and limitations. You can choose to be either the victim or creator of your life. The choice you make will determine the level of health and evolution you will experience. The quantum model empowers you. It assists you in making step-ups in your consciousness. The quantum model insists that you are actively involved in your own healing. The orthodox model keeps you subordinate to its hierarchy, as it sees you as a larva, while the quantum model views you as the butterfly!

The higher levels of Consciousness need to slow down their vibrations to allow for the collapse into the physical base level. At the base linear level, the tasks have been simplified into simple operations. Yet, it is very difficult to explain through lower-level behavior the activities of the multi-fold causation in the higher hierarchy because the linear concepts do not apply to the nonlinear behaviors. All the levels which are strongly bound internally interact with one another to make sure the desired outcome is produced. These are the reasons it is so important that in healing spiritually or physically, you do not take the physical as the dominant and singular cause and concentrate merely on just this symptom as happens in the western model. Rather, you need to look at the web of influences and multiple causes in the development of any imbalance as directed by the quantum downward causation model. In this way, when you look at a problem, you are able to see different levels of meaning in your problem. You cannot get this information from the orthodox model of upward causation alone because its information is very limited to the base level; and, therefore, it does not provide sufficient conditions nor higher level possibilities because of its limitations. Healings must happen at all levels and especially at the level of Consciousness. Then when you reach this level, the world becomes a meaningless nothing as you revel in total bliss. It is critical that you unite the diverse disciplines of the physical world and consciousness, as complementary aspects of the same reality of healing with the hope that eventually order will come out of the chaos.

In the downward causation model, the chakras play an important part in the balance and health of your body. The chakras, the spine of your Consciousness, are power and energy transformation routers that connect and transmute energy throughout the five levels of Consciousness, supramental, mental, vital and the physical. This is the architecture of your soul where healing takes place through these chakras in a multifactorial process. These five levels are connected through these putative energy centers, the chakras, positioned in the axis of your spinal column. Your Consciousness is an expanding and contracting force, expanding in its vortexal structure in a macrocosmic manner and contracting in a microcosmic universe. Quantum medicine, therefore, recognizes you as a regenerative, evolutionary system of Infinite Creative Intelligence.

Understanding through the quantum life model the continuity of your Consciousness, and how your Consciousness is woven into every second of your existence, will help you to support your dying process as well on the energetic level. This, in turn, will reduce your survival fear as well and assist you to conclude this life cycle awake with an attitude of calm positiveness, serene acceptance and full awareness by releasing you from the fear of death. Furthermore, by using reiki, another energy modality, rather than opioids, you can help bring peace to individuals as they interact with the transition of death.

You can clearly see how quantum medicine is involved in your care from the moment of birth to your moment of transitioning into another dimension not just in a fifteen-minute (if you are lucky) office visit. Quantum medicine operates from very different assumptions than the conventional model regarding the workings of your body. It looks at disease from an energetic spiritual component with disease as a message for the individual. It takes off the lens of illusion from your inner sight and views your physiology nonsensorily which is quite distinct from what meets the eye. Western medicine on the other hand has no conception of the continual exchange of energy and Consciousness. Several allopathic physicians with whom I have had similar discussions regarding Consciousness and healing, related to me, "You might as well be speaking Japanese to me because I have no idea about what you are talking. I cannot comprehend it. It goes right past me. All I know are drugs and surgery." The task at hand for quantum medicine is to bring the perceptions of western medicine that are mired in petty narrowness and shortsightedness into alignment with the quantum model, informed by quantum physics, that is broader and more inclusive. Together we can direct our collective dream.

The architectural structure of Consciousness is this: Consciousness-supramental-mental-vital-physical. This is the entire panoply of your life in which different aspects of Consciousness are viewed from their component parts. This is the entire rendition of the score of the Master. Consciousness is your divine Source which is imperishable; and the physical, which perishes at the end of every birth, is a vesture for Consciousness with the other dimensions bridging between the two. Consciousness is the Source that appears through the media of the gross and the subtle. Health and life are interdimensional in scope.

As we have discussed before, there are varying degrees of vitality amongst these downward causation dimensions of Consciousness-supramental-mental-vital-physical with causation initiated from the macro to the micro. If Consciousness is the Source and is Collective, then supramental is the diffused illumination of Consciousness into the Soul which is now beginning to individualize in its descent into the gross physical body. The mental is the mind and separate from the physical organ brain and a part of the transcendent world, not the physical world, and is the over-arching commander of the vital force; the vital is where your feelings and emotions are stored and out of which the morphogenetic field operates, holds its blueprints, and moves energy; then the physical is the gross body and follows suit from the vital body. When all the other bodies drop off, Consciousness is. The implicate order is primary. The energy from these different levels trickles from the top-down not bottom-up and they are immune to time. Time is only a product of the third dimension. As you increase your Consciousness, you will evolve into greater individuation.

The Quantum energy/medical/spiritual system is very dynamic and constantly changing and is not a stable fixed thing. Energy and communication between the levels can happen instantly without a visible linear pathway. A large quantum sudden non-sequential jump, discontinuity, occurs with nonlocal signals amongst these dimensions. In the descriptive sense all the levels of consciousness are different, but in the dynamic sense they are one despite that they are fifth and fourth dimensional, except for the physical level, which is third dimensional. They each have a life of their own and varying degrees of vitality but they are interconnected.

Health, therefore, needs to be addressed from all these levels and not just the physical which is the focus of conventional medicine's upward causation model. Furthermore, because western medicine is stuck in the "rat stage of science" and draws its conclusions from the third dimensional state, and ignores the fourth and fifth dimensions, then the data they acquire is inadequate and inconclusive. We are informed of this by quantum physics. With improper data, one cannot draw proper conclusions. As a result, western medicine has taught us very little about health enhancement and self-potentiation because it focuses on disease and singularity. Singularity, considered to be a merit in the physical third dimensional world, is an unknown quality in the fourth dimensional world because the spiritual world functions in one accord. Quantum energy/medicine/spirituality teaches "big medicine" in that it teaches personal capacity, strength and power. You are a hybrid being. You live in two worlds simultaneously – the third dimensional physical world and the fourth dimensional spiritual world both propelled by the Force of Consciousness, the causal body and fifth dimension.

MORPHIC RESONANCE AND ARCHETYPES

Your morphogenetic fields, or m–fields, are intriguing because they are nonlinear, spaceless, timeless, in inexorable flux and follow the downward causation model of quantum energy/medicine/spirituality. They cannot be confirmed to everyone's comfort in laboratory experiments because the m–fields have their residence in the astral and not the material. Morphic fields are vibratory and rhythmic activities that are not stored in the brain but in areas beyond the physical brain. These fields of vibratory activity come into form at a particular frequency once enough bits of information are attracted together. They are also not stored in the genes but in the morphic resonance of the previous species Dr. Amit Goswami has instructed us. They do collapse into matter through morphic resonance.

Morphic resonance according to Rupert Sheldrake, a British biologist, is a "nonlocal and creatively discontinuous influence by which a form can subsequently facilitate itself in a similar pattern because of the memory inherent, not just in the original form, but because of the collective memory of our universe." The morphic fields maintain the integrity of the original form, in an energetic blueprint, and maintain its probabilistic organizing abilities, Dr. Amit Goswami further instructed. This position, one would think, is very similar to that of Carl Jung and the collective unconscious, or Ervin Laszlo's cosmic memory in that memories are shared amongst and influence individuals close up or at a distance. The repetition of these shared memories seems similar to what Jung referenced as archetypes. Where Sheldrake and Jung part ways is that Jung believed the memories are shared through physical means in a mechanistic way such as through inheritance, while Sheldrake's position is one of discontinuity and nonlinearity and evolutionary.

Basically memory is present in all of nature. Once a precedence has been set of this morphogenesis, it is much more likely to occur again. When you collapse a new form through the work of your Consciousness, this new form sets up its own energetic field as a blueprint separate and independent from your physical form. It is actualized from a wave of possibilities through your vital subtle body into your physical body. M-fields, therefore, are templates of light and sound, non-local and non-energetic, from your Consciousness that collapse through your vital and physical into material form. These fields are a process of projection from your thought Mind and injection into your Vital body where your inner blueprints are housed and must be strong enough to be collapsed into the physical. The aetheric field has a template of every organ of your body which with focused intention and persistence and hard work you can download/ collapse to replace/heal a diseased organ.

You do not need to know how the blueprint works, but only that it is there and that you have this potential. Whatever may happen let us say to your physical organs, the energetic blueprints will always still be there and can be activated through the meta-blueprint. With pure intention your m-fields can give a signal to your DNA to activate a new form via the vibration and rhythm of morphic resonance instructed Dr. Amit Goswami, an enlightened physicist, and Dr. Paul Drouin, an awakened medical physician, both quantum giants. It is the intention, recognition, and choice that results in Consciousness amplifying the intention into the vital body which houses the blueprints, and collapsing the intention in a quantum leap to these meta-forms stored in the vital body from the many waves of possibilities from transcendent potentia, or quanta, into actuality. It has to be observed to collapse, and at that point there is only one choice. Until it is observed, there are many possibilities and these possibilities have many probabilities, which exist as waves. The electron here is in a state of potentia. Your awareness creates a quantum entanglement between Consciousness and the object that you choose to be involved with this phenomenon. This energetic blueprint is not fixed but continues to evolve and can have a global influence. This supports purposeful regeneration of quantum origin because of the memory that is exhibited in morphogenesis providing a remarkable opportunity for you to regenerate new pathways for your healing.

Sheldrake's theory of morphogenetic fields is a bold departure from anything envisioned or supported by convention or orthodoxy. Furthermore, morphogenesis is the biggest threat to the dying establishments. Yet, in quantum medicine, Sheldrake will always be remembered as a pioneer of hope and hope is biological. One can easily see why quantum medicine has embraced m-fields into its many quanta of healing opportunities.

M-fields have social implications as well as they organize fields around groups of people. They connect you while miles apart and allow you to communicate at a distance as one does through telepathy which is a normal, rather than paranormal, experience. Telepathy, direct communication of thoughts between minds, occurs frequently amongst people who know one another even at great distances. Telepathy and clairvoyance and remote viewing have been used and exploited by both the CIA in the United States and the Soviet Union to acquire and describe information about targets that were blocked from normal perception. The United States was able to identify with significant accuracy where Russian missiles were hidden. The governments have trained individuals to highly exploit this field of Consciousness for their own interests. These are all further experiences of our oneness and how we can even assist in one another's healing drawing on the pool of Consciousness.

NEUROPLASTICITY AND HOPE

Life changes. Accept it. It is what it is. It is this moment that matters. As hard as it may be at times, tell yourself this moment matters, I was rhetorically imparting to a colleague over lunch one day. We are both healthcare professionals. She is a physician and I am a psychologist. We were discussing the importance of sitting with our patients in their moment of suffering rather than just treating a disease. We both understand the alchemy of presence. You sit and you listen. You wait for them to find their wholeness within themselves and assure them that even in their brokenness there is the sacred.

With philosophical calm, we discussed the hopelessness of the chronically ill, and how lack of hope is a type of violence because it creates a paralysis of will on the individual's mind, since any healing process is initiated as a product of Consciousness. Consciousness is all there is we agreed. It is the ground of your being. There is nothing but Consciousness. Everything is initiated from Consciousness. Quantum medicine as informed by quantum physics instructs us how energy and communication between the interacting systems can happen instantly without a visible linear pathway. A large quantum sequential jump, or discontinuity, occurs with non-local signals among these dimensions.

My colleague then remarked passionately, "I do not believe that as physicians we should give a prognosis to our patients because once they have it, they want to do what the doctor told them will happen." Without realizing, my colleague was discussing quantum entanglement. When a doctor and a patient fail to act as a unit, together they become dysfunctional. But when one is in touch with one's own inner sovereignty and pair this authenticity with a spoken hopefulness, this will jumpstart the patient out of limitations and spiritual emptiness. The doctor's awareness then becomes the eyes through which the patient begins to see the physical world.

Observations of potential can be transformative because empowering others is the biggest gift we have to give. This unified Consciousness becomes like a pendulum downplaying one level and highlighting another.

I shared with my colleague the same view about the damage that comes with broadcasting a perceived prognosis and provided an experience of a family member who was recently diagnosed with very advanced esophageal cancer. Whenever the physician wanted to give Mark the prognosis, he put up his hand and insisted, "I don't want to know it. This is not the end I can assure you. This is only the beginning. I will survive this." Mark knew at some very deep level that where fear exists, healing cannot. He sensed that if he changed his thinking, he could change his life course - - epigenetics at its best. Blood composition controls the genetic response of the cells, and thoughts affect blood composition, which then affect cells.

Mark's cancer ravaged his esophagus and lymph nodes with a very large cancerous tumor perched between his stomach and esophagus. On the seemingly hopeless day of January 24th, an MRI showed no change after intensive chemotherapy and radiation in Mark's grave and very advanced esophageal cancer. On that same day, I segued myself into Mark's healing process and began a crash course with him, remotely, in alternate nostril breathing to aid in bringing both sides of his body into balance, primordial sound meditation to affect the cellular level, and reiki, activities to which Mark had no exposure. No further reliance on machines and drugs, but Consciousness. Then in the spirit of quantum entanglement, I instilled hope by continuously reassuring Mark that once he meditates and treats himself with reiki daily, that his physicians were going to be most surprised when they opened him for surgery. There is no such thing as false hope!

On February 13th, three weeks after the last MRI showed no change in the imaging results, Mark's surgery took place and surprised they were! His medical team found no sign of a tumor, no cancer in his lymph nodes, and only a small section of his esophagus needed to be surgically excised with anastomosis. Confident expectation of a cure does what no medical treatment will ever accomplish. Mark had eradicated his cancer by partnering with Consciousness through two quantum technologies, meditation and reiki, and shifted the paradigm! He used his mind and hands as a jumper cable to connect the circuitry and rebuild the grid. His pathology report also showed no sign of cancer.

Mark was stronger than his misfortunes. While his physical form took time to make the changes, his mind changed instantly and envisaged the direction in which it needed to go and coach the body. Mark made changes in neural pathways due to changes in his thinking and behavior – neuroplasticity in action! I recall Mark saying to me regarding the quantum energy healing modalities, "What did I have to lose!?" He said he felt empowered to be able to participate in his own healing "….and I honestly believe I could feel changes taking place in my body every time I meditated and performed reiki!"

These felt "shifts" were the clustering of atoms, as a result of his mind's intentions, which resulted in increased levels of energy vibrating within Mark's system. These shifts activated throughout the system began to create new connections for Mark, throwing off old negative imprints and creating new neural pathways. These higher energy flows created a reorganization, since the new patterns cannot be contained in the old structure.

Meditation became Mark's microscope for inner exploration. In this transcendent state, Mark became capable of profound change. He became pro-active and receptive. He became the causal agent of motion. He listened to his inner voice and refused to live in the straightjacket conventional assumptions surrounding his medical condition because he realized there was a dangerous blindness in accepting the prevailing view of society and that of the conventional medical community. This inner pollution is the collective disease of our planet. Being in the here and now transmutes the status quo. This moment matters! The more Mark meditated, the more he saw the limitations of the conventional conditioned mind. He modified, abandoned and transcended existing concepts.

Mark's mind became the artist that produced his wholeness. He walked through the doorway of his own integrity to support his healing with determination and perseverance. He was relentless in becoming self-active and self-sufficient. He refused to be reduced into a corporeal entity and absorb the psychotic limiting interpretations surrounding his condition imposed upon him by the dominant medical view. He knew he had super-sensible ideas of his own beyond the duality of psyche and soma. Self-determination, not external compulsion, is an idea that anticipates.

Mark played all the notes in his orchestra and brought about healing out of his chaos. He stopped outward gaze for direction and discursive chatter; and, rather, chose to draw on cellular potential and tapped into infinite possibilities. He dared to wake up from culture's hypnotic dogma, which renders a person into a trance and is one of disempowerment and limitations.

When Mark actively practiced reiki, an energy-based Consciousness hands–on healing technology that has the capability for tremendous personal healing and transformation, it resulted in major changes in his belief system. He offered that he could actually feel the healing come through the palms of his hands. As I treated Mark with reiki at the University of Michigan Medical Hospital after surgery, I watched the heart monitor go from 87 to a steady 65. As nursing staff watched Mark's monitors from their station, a family member overheard one nurse affirm, "Look at how relaxed Mark becomes during reiki!" The University of Michigan now readily makes reiki available for those who request it. Mayo Clinic uses reiki as a supportive healing modality to manage pain for patients during hemodialysis. They have seen the outcomes.

A study was done measuring the effect of healing touch on the properties of pH, oxidation–reduction balance, and electric resistance in body fluids. They linked these two factors to biological age only. The biologically determined age of the touch treated group before treatment was 62. However, after treatment for the same group, the biologically mathematically determined age was 49!

Reiki is a doorway into the healing world, but it also gives you greater control over your health and your destiny by opening to the limitless energy around you and channeling this energy through the palms of the hands to shift energy into the body. Reiki is guided by Consciousness to create depth, breadth, and natural healing. It came through Mark's heart in a simple and sincere manner.

The organization of reiki is holographic. In addition to using mind and breath, it also uses symbols as part of the healing process. Each symbol reflects the greater wisdom of the whole. Reiki with the symbols attunes you to a higher vibration. In reiki there is a power and focus symbol (cho ku rei), harmony and emotions symbol (sei hei ki), master and distance symbol (hon sha ze sho nen), kundalini symbol (dumo), and grounding and completion symbol (raku). These symbols are used for protecting and healing self and others on an emotional and spiritual level.

Unfortunately, this healing modality has become adulterated by numerous offshoots springing up, as to make reiki unrecognizable and complex. I taught reiki to Mark in its original simplicity. Reiki heals through stillness and simplicity. Mark gave it his wholehearted attention three times a day and became a bridge for transforming his body one cell at a time. Then he waited in stillness. The waiting was a tuning in, not tuning out. Mark became so lost in the silence, as he sat in a pool of Divine presence, that he became lost to everything else on Earth. His hands became the conduits for Consciousness. He became the instrument of ultimate artistic sensibility. All one needs is one experiential referent to make sense of reiki and its profound transformative healing energy.

Reiki plugged Mark into the energy dance of the Universe, a power so great that all other powers are a pale shadow beside it. Through reiki, Mark became the expression of the Infinite, the electromagnetic flux field of Universal Mind. The preludes and fugues of reiki healing are a complex arrangement of Divine Wisdom. I have successfully brought reiki back to its authentic simplified form and away from the "stamps," "twists", or "additions" that so many practitioners have added for financial gain. The simplified form is justly a course in enlightenment.

All healing is a product of Consciousness, and meditation and reiki healing are based on the science of physics, the study of energy directed by Consciousness and intention. They fuel a change in energy. It is a change that you, and only you, can create in yourself. An intention on your part alters the chemistry and energy of your being. Healing is not simply a product of medication and surgery. The latter are helpful symptom resolutions, but they are an incomplete approach that only treats the physical and not the quantum subtle bodies that are the downward manifestations of Consciousness from which all healing is initiated. Healing is a quantum phenomenon. Mark's experience exemplifies how quantum healing through mind, energy, and breath can be converted or transduced into another form. You hold within yourself the transformative and regenerative power to make yourself what you will. "Every human being is the author of his own health or disease," we are reminded by Buddha.

You have the ability to objectify any imbalance with the recognition that the imbalance is the priority of the material body and not Consciousness. With this understanding is how "miracles" take place. If you can get out of your own way and sit with your physical form in silence and talk to your organs, which store all the memories from your life, you would then achieve deep resonance with every cell and every organ and facia of your body. Exploiting the unlimited possibilities of meditation and reiki for healing, which are accessible to all and are non-invasive, you can create definitive changes from the cellular level all the way to all the major regulatory mechanisms, i.e. telomere length, inflammatory markers, and cell repair to name a few. This way, you affect the epigenetic landscape without becoming consumed with genes. You have a pluripotential environment in your body that is very fluid. You can readily affect it - - in silence. Sit in silence, talk to your organs, which have a Consciousness of their own. Then, just LISTEN to the voice of silence. The voice of the soul and the voice of silence is the breath! Follow the ins-and-outs of breath. Receive intuition and a knowing of what is needed. When you ask for what you need, there is a response.

Refuse to settle for a "normal" consciousness because failure can only occur if you create an antagonistic auto-suggestion as a result of doubt. Furthermore, do not be willing to wait for some external power to do the work for which you are responsible. Break away from herd mentality and infantile fixation. Consciousness lives in the timeless present and is available for your healing. Meditate to prepare yourself with an inner readiness so that you can become quiet enough to perceive this deep Source within yourself through the reiki work. Meditation and reiki are two time-honored systems which bring change and which are safe and inner-directed and often without the expense of other healing modalities. These two technologies require no expensive instruments, no invasive procedures nor pharmacological treatments.

Through these technologies you will admit new information which will form new neural connections and enlarge your awareness as you leap forward. You will display that there is no limit to your consciousness except those created by your own thinking! Your higher Consciousness has a perennial wisdom not explainable by atomic sensory means. It discloses that spatio-temporal limitations are merely optical illusions! The more you practice these technologies, the more you provoke growth and changes in the cellular and molecular structure of your body, and the more you form new neural pathways. Mark knew he was not a robot of medical limitations. He continues to be cancer free.

To maximize even further the benefits of reiki, one might want to pair up reiki with chronobiology, referring to the day-night cycle which affect the human body and which tells us that the flow of energy, chi, is best at specific times of the day. There tends to be a clock-like pattern of energy that moves through your different organs and associated meridians on a predictable two-hour cycle. A type of internal rhythm one might say. The time, perhaps, when the nutritive subtle life-energy is moving the best, might be the optimal time to treat a particular organ for maximum benefits. The precise timing of a treatment can have a more potent effect on the target organ. Groundbreaking research is now coming through on chronobiology and chronopharmacology. Chronobiology is finding its place in the fields of genetics, endocrinology, oncology, sports medicine and even psychology. The timelines for maximum energetic output look like this, Dr. Richard Gerber, M.D. in his book <u>Vibrational Medicine</u>, informs us:

<u>MORNING HOURS</u> to corresponding <u>EVENING HOURS</u>

1 to 3 a.m. = Liver	1 to 3 p.m. = Small Intestine
3 to 5 a.m. = Lung	3 to 5 p.m. = Bladder
5 to 7 a.m. = Large Intestine	5 to 7 p.m. = Kidney
7 to 9 a.m. = Stomach	7 to 9 p.m. = Heart Constrictor
9 to 11 a.m. = Spleen/Pancreas	9 to 11 p.m. = Triple Heater
11 a.m. to 1 p.m. = Heart	11 p.m. to 1 a.m. = Gall Bladder

If there is a specific focus on any particular organ, this chronobiological time calendar might be useful to consider if the times are at all feasible for the practitioner. For instance, if you are having stomach issues, doing reiki with yourself or acupuncture with a practitioner around 8 a.m. might be the most optimal time for the best therapeutic results.

Not only is being familiar with the chronobiological clock useful for merging reiki and acupuncture, but significant utility is being discovered for the administration of chemotherapeutic agents. Giving it at an optimal time might reduce toxicity levels for the cancer patient. At this point with its yet limited research, it is appearing that early morning hours may very well be the optimal time to administer cancer related drugs. This biological clock is certainly associated with our subtle energy systems. The more you learn about energy philosophies that are available to you from quantum medicine rather than conventional medicine, the more options you have for healing your body naturally and the more hope you provide yourself for natural organic healing. Return to healing with energy not drugs.

Let us not forget that hope is restorative and biological. Quantum medicine, quantum entanglement and neuroplasticity offer real hope. Hope and health go hand-in-hand. Something deep inside your cells responds positively when you feel hope. Hope is real and physiological and affects the immune system. People's beliefs about themselves affect their ability to get well. Despair, caused when an individual feels there can be no hope of solving his problem by his own actions, dissipates energy from the bodily storehouse in the brain without conscious direction poisoning all the different cellular groupings of which body organs are composed. On the other hand, hope empowers an individual and replaces the energy funds, as it is the antitheses of despair.

Hope extended to a patient allows the patient to see his issue in a different light, undo the imbalance and create a space for a different form. This discernible link between doctor and patient sets the stage for collaborative work. There is no higher or lower level, no hierarchy between doctor and patient. The movement goes back and forth between the two people to allow for a leap in healing by returning to the starting point, our original level – Oneness – by being together in the collective. Both blend and become one with each other so that the two create an endogenous oscillation of vibration and an intense relational space by synchronizing their nervous systems. It is a unitary experience of two people doctor and patient, from which limitless healing can take place. It is quantum entanglement enhancing neuroplasticity.

Health care professionals, therefore, must not barricade themselves with an invisible pretentious wall. We need to be open to the alchemy that happens in being together, the transformative chemistry that becomes the spiritual dance of life. My eyes became the eyes through which Mark saw himself, the physical world and his potential.

We need to shift from a reductionistic intervention of drugs and surgery, and move into an integrative quantum approach to health, which broadens the scope of recognizing cellular potential ignited by hope and awareness of our consciousness, and empowering and partnering, rather than dismissing, our patients. Miracles are a quantum phenomenon and available to all of us if we dare to wake up and let our embryonic Consciousness evolve from Homo Sapiens to Home Spiritualis. You have the potential for greatness and unlimited abilities. Do not keep yourself small. Rewire your brain by changing your thinking and redefining your awareness. There is a better way to live.

QUANTUM HEALING, QUANTUM LIFE

Quantum Healing is a simple notion with profound results. The body knows how to bring itself into balance and how to keep itself in balance in face of disease because your mind has Infinite Intelligence. True healing, therefore, takes you back to Source. Anything short of that is temporary. Furthermore, we must not forget that an illness is a path in its own right. It is your teacher and a great opportunity toward wholeness. An illness is pregnant with meaning and provides you the opportunity to Oneness itself.

You are learning about the different factors that make up what you finally can become, a spiritual being who has the ability to activate your Consciousness for your healing and access deeper layers of yourself to objectify imbalances by nurturing the infinite intelligence of your mind. Our society is hungry for a healing method that incorporates techniques and beliefs that address the whole being emphasized Dr. Paul Drouin, M.D. Dr. Drouin informs us in his book Creative Integrative Medicine that "we become ill when our cellular anatomic level does not have that sense of Sourceness and it is locked in rather than free."

The quantum healing model sees the individual as incomparable and inimitable. Western physicians must first do this work within themselves if they are going to facilitate whole person care and spiritual unfoldment in their patients by refining their own Consciousness to a higher vibratory frequency. You are not distilled in a pharmaceutical lab but in higher states of Consciousness. The quantum healing method is a Spirit-matter model that helps you awaken to your essence and create a fluidity in your consciousness. Although your expression is in a third atomic dimensional world, you are created in a higher frequency world which is non-atomic. Between the atomic (contracted movement of energy) and non-atomic (expanded self) is where you will gain the realization of infinite potential. You are both alpha (physical) and omega (infinite) simultaneously.

We have already discussed that healing is scientific and is a change in energy that only you can create. Someone else might facilitate this change, but you only can create the change within yourself. For years I have cherished and been inspired by *Herman Hesse's* poem that clearly exemplifies our self-empowerment:

> *I can give you nothing*
> *That has not already its*
> *Being within yourself.*
> *I can throw open to you*
> *No picture gallery but*
> *Your own.*
> *I help you to make*
> *Your own world visible.*
> *That is all.*

Therefore, health and disease are active processes of your mind. Health is the result of a harmonious mind and disease results from the disharmony of the mind. Recognizing this carries for you implicit responsibility and opportunity. When you participate in the process of your own health, no matter how unconsciously, then you can overcome your own disease. Pierre Teilhard de Chardin, a priest scientist who has moved me profoundly in my spiritual evolution, and who was filled with reverence for the material world but never lost sight of the spiritual, instructs us, "The ills from which we are suffering have their seat in a foundation of thought." He emphasized our connectivity and remarked how difficult it is to think any other way but collectively. Paramahansa Yogananda in his book <u>The Autobiography of a Yogi</u> instructed that "whatever your powerful mind believes very intensely instantly comes to pass."

Therese Neuman, a German Catholic mystic and stigmatic, exemplified the power of her mind as she materialized "spontaneous" healings both in her blindness and appendicitis. She then displayed *inedia,* the ability to live without food and water, and did so for thirty-five years while observed being totally sustained by the Eucharist. She submitted herself to numerous very strict medical evaluations and observations and was not left alone for a single moment day and night to ensure accurate medical research findings. She was periodically weighed and blood smears were done and her bowels evaluated. The latter eventually stopped. She also showed no signs of dehydration despite having given up water as well. No weight was lost except the first few days when her stigmata would open and would regain the weight quickly thereafter. The tests were conclusive that Therese Neuman did not eat or drink but was sustained by the energy of her thoughts, prana, air and sunlight and materialized whatever she needed internally energetically.

Prahlad Jani, an Indian Breatharian, also lived without food and water since 1940. He transitioned in May, 2020 and claimed he was sustained energetically by his goddess Amba. He was kept under medical supervision in a hospital where he was observed twenty-four hours a day for an extended period of time. He was continuously observed by medical experts and was being viewed under camera. He was under constant surveillance. It was concluded that no food nor water was taken by Prahlad Jani and he did not lose his energy nor his mental capacities.

These are not isolated cases as now there is a sizable number of individuals practicing Breatharianism globally and who believe without a shadow of a doubt that they can live on prana, air and sunlight to sustain their life. They know that their vital force is within them and all around them and can feed every cell of their body. Before such individuals embark on such a journey, they do extensive work to open up their prana centers. It is a very advanced spiritual awakening, and I do not recommend Breatharianism, without extensive preparation and supervision, as it could be fatal and some have died in such an attempt. I also find it unnecessary for spiritual evolution. Significant preparation and objectives must be undertaken to prepare the body for such undertaking. It does show the power of our mind and the ability of our energetic subtle system to live on its own energy alone however. The energetic body is a wondrous beautiful composition.

Let us briefly look at some of the principles and physics of energy in order that you may better understand the science of your quantum life. Furthermore, the more you understand atomic energy, the more you understand yourself. Understanding atomic energy is one thing; making use of it is another.

Basically, all matter consists of atoms. Atoms are made up of tiny particles. Yet every particle contains all the other particles as informed by quantum physics. It can be proven mathematically but hard to visualize or understand. The universe and everything in it is matter. However, there is no intelligence in matter except that which has been crystallized through the Energy Source of your Consciousness. This is very similar to an automobile. The automobile has no intelligence save what the driver tells it to do. Whatever the driver tells it, it follows orders. Your Consciousness is the driver to your physical body which is merely an aggregate of protons and electrons. These particles are the same in every type of atom, although their numbers vary. For example, a butterfly and you are both made of atoms. What makes one a butterfly and the other you is the different number of particles inside your various atoms that combine to create them. The basic patterns are the same but different energy constitutions.

The idea of one particle containing the all is best implied in William Blake's famous verse:

> *To see a world in a grain of sand*
> *And a heaven in a wild flower,*
> *Hold infinity in the palm of your hand,*
> *And eternity in an hour.*

Atoms are the ultimate independent units of your being. Yep, you are atomic! Atoms, although an associated structure of the physical third dimension, receive their regenerative power from the fourth/fifth dimension. The fourth/fifth dimensions are transmitters. Your physical body is the receiver. You can short-circuit this transfer of information between transmitter and receiver and cause a breakdown, perhaps, by your negative thoughts or by some psychic or physical damage in the component parts.

The more your atoms are confined, the more they move around. They resist confinement. When your atoms collide, the energy of the two colliding atoms creates particles which redistribute to form a new pattern. These particles identified as protons (positively charged +), electrons and neutrons (negatively charged -), live for a short time and disintegrate to again reconstitute into other subatomic particles. They are created from energy and vanish into energy, since energy cannot be destroyed but only transformed.

Now this is where you may want to read and re-read until it is clear. Since thought is also energy and energy has always existed and will continue to exist, then thoughts have always existed. As your thoughts surface, they register as a sine wave (a frequency energy wave), oscillating energy throughout the body. The higher its frequency, the more peaks and troughs it has. The lower frequency becomes a flatter wave. These sine waves are characteristic of everything and are patterns of potentia. You can feel this shift in energy in your body as Mark did when he was doing reiki. When you focus your thoughts with intention, the atoms react to their confinement with motion and come closer to the surface of awareness. So now your atoms are becoming very excited, and the frequency or number of waves made in one second increases. Now you have yourself functioning at a higher level of frequency. In thoughts, that are out of your awareness, at a distance, the atoms will be more spaced out and the frequency of the sine wave is decreased because they are less concentrated and less excited. All waves, whether distant or closer, cover the same distance but they will vibrate and oscillate differently.

Now here is the deal: When you have two waves that are the same frequency and direction and peak and trough at the same time, you are now "in phase." The combined amplitude of two "in phase" waves is larger than a single wave because it is carrying more information than one wave and carries with it great power in terms of the energy to accomplish common goals. This "in phase" process of sine waves gives you a behind-the-scenes view of what happens in quantum entanglement.

Do consider what this is saying to you. When you have the same positive thought and continue to build on it repeatedly or meditate with a partner holding the same intention, you will carry great power. But when you keep changing your mind, or you and a partner are at odds in terms of your goals, the amplitude of the resultant wave is zero, actually smaller than that of the waves before they meet. In fact, they cancel each other's energy. This is called destructive interference in physics. In <u>The Quantum Life,</u> I call it oppositional polarity because you are giving up energy by opposing it or by your partner opposing it. You are always starting over, because the opposing thought disrupts the flow of current, energy, through the circuits of your mind. A break in your circuits stops current from flowing smoothly or at all.

See what implications this all has for your life. In your life you will have certain repetitive thoughts or experiences that will create a build-up of energy. If you do not release these thoughts, especially if they are negative thoughts, you will have static energy that gets confined and eventually create either a physical or mental illness. You need meditation, reiki, psychotherapy, exercise or some modality for the release of this built-up static energy. If this static energy builds up so high to disturb your equilibrium, your atoms will have a nuclear explosion named cancer or psychotic illness or depression or fibromyalgia. The agony of your spirit will always be reflected in your bodily function.

Let us go further now and say that you have so much love in your heart to give out but cannot seem to find an outlet. Well, you might say love, a frequency, is good. Love is GOoD. However, this build-up has the potential to create static energy as well if you have no outlet for all the love. Yet, every *act* of love releases blocked energy in the atoms of your body. Stop being satiated with yourself and turn your focus outward in the service of your fellow man. Give selfless service to all without prejudice. My own personal sacred contract is a life of service.

Get out and do volunteer work or become involved in community projects. You can also send out long-distance healing energy through reiki and discharge some of that love. Try meditation as well for sending out love. To do this you will bring your energy up from muladhara, your tailbone chakra, up to sahasrara, crown chakra, then take it into the heart chakra and direct it to your goal. More on the chakras further on in the book. After extensive research, the Heart Math organization informs us that the energy of the heart travels at a 138,000 miles per second and never stops. Distance places no barricade in long distance healing. Fire out that love!

Love transforms and physics has informed us that life can only be understood in terms of relatedness. Things are nothing in isolation and atoms transform only in relation to other atoms. The mansion of your soul is built out of the brick of relationships provided by others for your use. You either love or you perish! The glory of life consists on your ability to feel deeply and experience widely.

Love was inspired by immortal hope but it requires mortal effort to keep it alive and in action. You do this by turning your allegiance from self to mankind as a whole. Transcend yourself and become a link in the electromagnetic force of humanity. When you can link yourself with chains of love to the Master Builders you will truly be performing the spiritual dance of life to an incredible and unforgettable symphony. "Practice love until you remember that you are love." Swami Sai Premananda.

I have always found of value Harry Stack Sullivan's, a world-renowned psychiatrist, definition of love. In paraphrasing, he states that love is when the needs of the other person become as important as your own. There is no hierarchy in love. Love then is the active concern for the growth of the person whom you love. When you love someone, you will help that person realize himself by providing opportunities. Love is progressive not demanding. Pressuring another to do what you want that person to do does not lead toward an expansion of your consciousness. Pressure, clutching, and possession diminish your spiritual energy. Even if that person would do what you wanted him to do, he will cringe inwardly. The victory is a failure for your soul. When you are in good terms with yourself, you will manifest an increase in spontaneous goodwill toward others. On the flip side, as long as you stay an automaton, you cannot love. Let go of expectations and don't be so over-determined or you will be lonely and psychologically naked in the world that will never weave a garment of love for you. You will relentlessly drive yourself into a spiritual vacuum. Rather, stand back once a process has been energized and formed. Let it take its course. When you have no expectations, you will be at peace. Love can only come from the pureness of your heart. It comes from the quietude of your consciousness. Love is all that matters.

Love is not an exceptional-individual phenomenon. It is a state of absolute and unconfined frequency of energy accessible to everyone in the midst of every experience. The drive to love the world is an inevitable facet of our spiritual maturation. Love must be experienced not in thought, but in the act, in the experience of oneness. Love in action, therefore, is the predominant proof of an individual's understanding of interdimensional physics understanding of the reality of life and death, and understanding of the importance of changing negative biases, which are the functioning basis of the subconscious, by changing the falsity of a particular belief.

Meditate on love as your interdimensional bridge. It is an action in the mood of eternity not linear time. Love is the root of your creative spirit which relates you to the unbounded Spirit. Without love you are stuck in the quicksand. Love is your lifeline. It is trans-spatial and trans-temporal. In every act of love you mold yourself. This is Love's dance with Itself. Fall in love with your Consciousness!

You can see how your evolution is concerned with every thought you think. Every thought you think is a reflection of your spirit, your higher frequency. Your mind is your spirit, which lives in a higher dimension than that of your brain. Your senses are the temporal source of supply for the content of your spirit mind. Therefore, you make or unmake yourself with your thoughts. Your life will be richer or poorer for the thoughts you have today. You are the master, molder, maker, and shaper of your soul which gets reflected in your health. You hold within yourself the transforming and regenerative power to make yourself what you will. Your present circumstances have grown out of the thoughts which you secretly harbor. In life you attract what you are not what you want. Read these words carefully again. *In life you attract what you are not what you want.* Look around and see what you have attracted. If you don't like what you see, change your thoughts, change your life. Become that which you want to attract. When a negative thought pops up, as they so often do, and wants to continue to victimize you, tell it that it is a part of the old self and no longer needed nor wanted. Tell it that it does not fit into your new true self which is the spirit-filled Self. Note that your body will always respond to your thoughts. Break and form new patterns by new thoughts, by admitting new information, which enlarges your awareness, and you will then leap forward.

THE SUBTLE SPIRITUAL SPINE

Chakras are highly charged circular energies centers of light that exist in your subtle bodies and regulate your physical body as they are aligned with the seven main endocrine glands. When in balance the chakras are filled with life force. Western scientists have more recently taken greater interest in these vortexes of energy. The chakras, a cohesive energy field, are the system of your energetic body or the inner organs of your esoteric system and feed your organs at its source. They are situated in a descending vertical line from your crown to your tailbone. I call the chakras your inner subtle spine and you can learn to take your cues from these sacred pulses of subtle energies as you learn to communicate with your body. They vibrate from the inside out and bring energy from the outside in as they radiate this information through your skin. They are a never-ending flow of energy. The chakras are also often viewed as organs of psychic perception especially the ajna chakra which is the sixth chakra in the middle of the forehead. As you master each of the individual chakras, you ascend toward the Divine. Each one helps you to refine your understanding of your spiritual power. Violating your spirit weakens the chakras and diminishes your body. It is through these "roots" that you fuel your body not through any other origin. Do not wait for a personal earthquake to trigger your ascent into your Divinity. Listen to your gut instinct because that is your survival message which comes from your chakras. They are the gateway into your internal world. Breathe health, spirit, and power into your chakras and "believe as if it were true now" the Book of Daniel instructs us.

Chakras

Energy enters your body through the root and crown chakras. In between these two chakras are five other major chakras. As you ascend upward in your mastery of the chakras, you gain in spiritual and self-power. The chakras take energy from higher dimensional regions and translate them into your hormonal and glandular system. This transfer of energy is reflected in your physical body. Illness is a depletion in one of these chakras. A depletion in any one of these chakras will show as pathology in your physical body. For instance, depletion in your throat, or fifth chakra, can show up as either hyper or hypothyroid. At this point, we have significant research that reflect evidence of the existence of the chakra system. When you develop and advance in your consciousness, you will be able to transfer and transmit energy through these chakras at will. The chakras are a part of the electromagnetic spectrum with different frequency which range higher as you ascend the spiritual spine.

The seven chakras, sacred ancient imagery, are all connected together as a complete system with nadis (fine threads of subtle energy which form a pathway) to the sushumna. The nadis are an extensive network of channels totaling approximately 72,000. They are interwoven within your physical nervous system. The sushumna runs along the central axis of your body within your spine between your crown and your sacrum. The *sushumna*, which represents consciousness, connects all the chakras. It has its physical counterpart with your central nervous system. On the right (masculine) side of the *sushumna* is the *pingala* channel which influences the left side of the brain and right side of your body. It carries with it plenty of solar energy and heat to warm your body and corresponds with your sympathetic nervous system. It is also full of drive. It begins at the right-hand side of the Root chakra and ends at the right nostril. The left (feminine) side is the *ida* channel which influences the left side of your body and the right hemisphere of your brain and provides you cool and calm lunar energy. It begins on the left-hand side of the root chakra and ends at the left nostril. *Ida* and *pingala* wind their way around your spinal cord through the *sushumna* like a serpent, crisscross at each chakra, and meet at the nose which is the 6th chakra. In the *sushumna* is where your life energy is concentrated. *Ida* is the left side feminine negative moon and *pingala* is the right side masculine positive sun. *Ida* and *pingala* govern the autonomic nervous system and *sushumna* governs the central nervous system.

A great way to balance both sides of your body and brain hemispheres is to do *alternate nostril breathing* which I have been practicing for at least thirty-five years. It puts you in balance and calibrates your life-field. First exhale heavily through both nostrils several times. Then press the right nostril with your thumb and then inhale from the left nostril which activates *ida* and imagine energy from the earth coming up your spine; for a second, keep both nostrils pressed, and raise your eyes between the eyebrows. Hold it for a second. Exhale and imagine energy in the subtle realms going down your spine. Then inhale from right nostril which activates *pingala*. Press the right nostril after your inhale. Hold it for a second, to attune yourself to pure spirit, and look upward between your eyebrows. At this point exhale from both nostrils several times which activates *sushumna*, the central channel, and bring that pure spirit energy down all your chakras. Keep repeating this pattern to attune your entire body. Initially only do this healing balancing exercise for a couple of minutes because you may get dizzy. After some experience, you may increase your time as you choose. It is relaxing and energizing at the same time. I especially like to do alternate nostril breathing after I have been on a flight while travelling. It quickly brings my body into balance. If you are having difficulty sleeping, do left nostril breathing to activate the relaxing *ida* and the right hemisphere. Cover the right nostril to block the active *pingala* and shut down the active left brain and activate the calming *ida* and the right relaxing side of your brain. You are now beginning to harness the vital energy of your body. Try alternate nostril breathing next time you feel tired rather than a cup of coffee. It works. Try it.

There are seven main chakras. At the crown you have the 7th crown chakra (sahasrara) at the top of your skull; between your brows you have the 6th chakra (ajna) and is located above your physical eyes in center of forehead; the 5th chakra is around the throat (vishuddha) and is in your lower neck; the 4th heart chakra (hridaya) behind the breast bone; 3rd solar plexus chakra (manipura) between the breast bone and the belly button; 2nd sacral chakra (swadisthana) which is two inches below the navel; and then the 1st root chakra (muladhara) between the tailbone and the pubic bone, in the groin. These seven chakras, energy vortexes, make up your spiritual spine in your human body through which Divine energy, prana, passes. Prana is your life force and is working behind every subtle mechanism in your body. The chakras are the most active at dawn and dusk and therefore useful to meditate during these times when possible. These are times when you can bathe in the bliss of your divine consciousness.

Although the chakras are fixed in your central spinal column, they are on both the front and back of your body and work through it. They close and open and expand and retract. They are team players and help one another. If one chakra begins to close down, another chakra will take over until the former gets back its strength. However, this expansion cannot last for too long or it will stress all the chakras. By beginning to communicate with your chakras you will begin to peel the layers of your being and reveal your inner depths that lie within you. You will start from the physical and eventually meet the transcendental. Once you start from the physical, the next step will open up to you. Be aware of the first chakra moment to moment, then ascend upwards to the crown chakra. Start where you are. Then reach where you can be which is feeling your body from the inside out. You will become acquainted with your inner geography. You know your body as others see it. But do you know your body as you can see it in an unsharable way. Integrity and honor are important characteristics for healthy balanced chakras. Chakra communication takes you from what you do to what you *are* because there can be no health without honor.

I have a young friend of great honor and integrity who was in significant emotional pain because of the way she was potentially going to recant certain vows. However, the way she was feeling was distorted and not necessarily true reality, although certainly her personal emotional reality in that moment. She was significantly neglected emotionally in a marriage by her partner. Her loneliness caused her to consider alternatives because she realized that nothing in her world was working least of all her marriage. As frightening as it was to leave her marriage, she did so, despite placing herself in a most vulnerable financial position. Yet her spiritual maturity supported her in freeing her spirit despite entering a very dark period in her life and significantly challenging her heart chakra. In this freedom, she saw the parameters of her husband's true character in their separation. Remember that life is never open for judgment because judgment is a spiritual error. It misses the mark rather than hitting the mark. However, because this most sensitive and bright female doctor perceived herself as having compromised her honor by considering other options, she was making herself emotionally very ill and was becoming quite neurotic with shame and guilt. I asked her to begin work on cleansing her chakras, alter her way of thinking about her life and choices, take specific herbs before breakfast, and soak in mineral baths. She has now made a commitment to her own healing. I am noticing that the stronger her spirit is becoming the less authority her marriage and her orthodox history are influencing her life. Orthodoxy can be a source of great pain when we reflect on our past; yet it is also an opportunity for new choices and new beginnings. It does require a revolution to move away from group thought. This revolution is placing my young friend in a position to influence her own choices and to influence the next stage of her life in a way that is meaningful to her. Her discomfort is now directing her to change her life one small step at a time. Her revolution has shifted to personal involution, the exploration of her inner self. There is nothing simple about my friend's journey, as she certainly has had to nurture her wounded child within from years of repressed emotional data. However, she is healing her pain rather than marketing her pain, as she redefines herself beyond her role as wife. I know her human spirit can transcend any limitation. A larger dynamic is moving through her or otherwise this Universal "scheme" would not have taken place in her life. Chance, or unintended event, is an illusion. Nothing in life happens by accident. Despite her discomfort, she recognizes that all things begin and end at appropriate times, and that a new beginning follows this chapter in her life. She is stretching her parameters.

I remember, as well, many years ago meeting for the first time the wife of a business associate. She shook my hand and within ten seconds informed me that she was a sexual abuse survivor. Her introduction of herself took me by surprise, and I wondered for some time why this woman wanted me to know her wounds so quickly, and what acknowledgment or supportive response she may have wanted from me for these historical pains. She continued to inform me that she has been in therapy for many years, but obviously she was not healing her wounds. She was merely marketing them and branded herself with this experience. She had allowed herself to become extremely invested in the authority of her pain and the sexual abuse became her identity and social currency. I noticed that same evening this woman knew no other pattern of interaction socially by which to connect with others except through her wounds as a lift-off. I overheard this woman repeat the same ritual, as she had with me, numerous times with others throughout the evening noting that this marketing had become her full time life-style and career. This woman's lower four chakras were significantly out of balance and harmony. She especially needed to call her spirit back by empowering her heart chakra. Love is the absence of fear. Where fear exists love cannot.

You feel the way you think. You change the way you think and you change the way you feel. Try the following internal exercise with yourself. As you are feeling a particular way, and if you do not like the way you are feeling at the moment, think differently about the situation, and notice what happens to your feeling. Try thinking three different ways now just for practice and notice how feelings change immediately. You will quickly learn how your thoughts generate your emotions, and stay attuned to understanding the energy consequence of every thought you generate.

The chakras, which contain spiritual life lessons, have colors associated with them and eventually with regular practice you will be able to see their colors. The crown chakra is purple (or white) and is in the ultraviolet spectrum. These colors have a very high frequency and a short wavelength with high energy and high momentum. The brow chakra is indigo; throat chakra is sky blue; heart chakra is green; solar chakra is yellow; sacral chakra is orange and the root chakra is red with a low frequency and is in the infrared spectrum and a low wavelength with low energy and low momentum. The chakras follow the colors of the rainbow. You hold a rainbow within yourself!

Because the chakras vibrate in a color frequency, some individuals are very capable of reading the color and health of the chakras, but some others cannot. The reason is that our brain waves are in the range of 0 to 100 cycles per second (Hz) and chakras vibrate from 100 to 1600 Hz. Our brain is just not trained to read such high frequencies. However, through meditation we come closer to reading these frequencies. Meditation aids you to awaken kundalini energy in the root chakra. Kundalini is your total potential of your total possibilities. It is seeded in your root chakra, coiled and asleep like a serpent, and becomes erect when awakened. When your energy is awakened in unity, then you are experiencing kundalini, and the more meaningful life becomes because you will awaken your full potentia. It is a moment of explosion. Do not try to understand it from your brain because you will interfere with the transformation. Understand it from your solar plexus. This is your root. This is from where you originated. You must go back to your roots. Take the first step. It is all up to you. There is a better way to live.

You might have some surprises in your day-to-day activity in confronting chakra colors. I recall an incident I experienced while my husband and I attended a late summer music festival. We were walking by the lake and a seagull flew very close to us. I commented in awe and amazement to my husband, "What an incredible remarkably beautiful green seagull that is! I have never seen a green seagull." He looked at me with great surprise responding back, "That seagull is white as all seagulls are! It is pure white!" I begged him to look again and validate that it is green. He chuckled and humored me by looking one more time and reiterated with even stronger emphasis this time, "It is pure white!" I looked around at all the other seagulls on the lake and to me all the seagulls were green. I then realized I was seeing the energetic bodies of these seabirds and not their physical body!

There is considerable research that validates the chakras. The chakras can lead you to your spiritual evolution and enLIGHTenment. From a quantum perspective, your body is organized by this energy coming from the chakras. The way to activate any chakra is to concentrate on it. By concentrating on it you will create new energies which will be so subtle you will not feel it at all initially. Yet you will feel vitalized and re-energized and you will know something different is taking place. It is organic. It is bliss.

The three lower chakras are the physical chakras connected to the energy of the mother earth and often associated with power and a sense of well-being and security. They are calibrated to external power so that boys are usually pushed toward these three chakras. Most of humankind is stuck in the first two lower chakras. The three upper chakras are the spiritual chakras associated with healing, awareness, and spiritual expression; and the heart chakra, toward which girls are directed, is associated with love and morals and bridges both the upper and lower chakras. Most people rarely get beyond the heart chakra. Between the crown and brow chakra is where most of your spiritual journey will take place in your consciousness. I typically rise immediately into my third eye during my meditations and survey the spiritual landscape from this vantage point. These upper four chakras are calibrated toward internal power. We must not let the upper or lower to dominate, but to integrate them together.

Ajna in the upper chakras is probably the most important of the chakras. It is often known as the eye of the Gods and reflected in the pineal gland just below the crown of the head. The pineal gland has a magnetostatic sensitivity, magnetic steady currents, and regulates the entire endocrine system. It is called pineal because it is in the shape of a pine cone. It functions like an antenna as an organism of sense perception and can be used as a special organ for acquiring knowledge. Its development is the emblem of divinity because an open pineal gland is a truth detector. Pineal gland produces melatonin and when it is inactive is when you experience insomnia as well as lack of intuition. When your pineal gland is closed, you can easily be deceived. On the other hand, an open pineal gland picks up on subtle inconsistencies. It is regarded as a link between the objective and subjective states of consciousness. It is your organ of conscious vision way beyond what your physical eyes can perceive. You begin to see with your inner eyes. With discipline you can reach your spiritual completeness by focusing on the 6th chakra, ajna, your invisible spiritual eye reflected through the visible pineal gland. When activated by focused intention on it, it shares and drips its nectar to the rest of the chakras below it. The chakra above it, the 7th chakra, sahasrara, reaches down for its own share. Your divinity exercises its function through this chakra more than the rest. When you concentrate on any one chakra you emit higher levels of photons which are quantum of light. The more awakened you keep your chakras, the more photons you will emit.

Most of you reading this book are aware of the sensitive area of the crown in a newborn called fontanel (soft spot). This area is right above the pineal gland, over the third eye, and because it stays open children often experience a long period of clairvoyance as this "openness" allows them to continue to live in the invisible worlds. This is also why they often remember their past lives until around eight years of age because they are still connected to the spiritual worlds through this opening. As the child develops, this crown area fully closes, and they become more oriented to the physical world.

Chakras are transformers of energy that influence both the cellular and organ level through the powerful endocrine system. The endocrine system affects the cellular system to our entire central nervous system. Imagine then the influence the chakras have on our hormonal body and consequently on brain activity. The chakras, which provide nutritive energy, are directly connected to your inner and outer emotional balance. This nutritive energy must be unimpeded to maintain the vitality of your physical body. Each of the chakras operate on a different frequency, and the frequency increases as you go higher, but each higher chakra continues to carry the frequency of the previous chakra and adds its own. You can enhance and/or balance any chakra merely by doing a chakra bath by visualizing the color associated with a chakra while meditating. Another way is to wear clothing that are the color of a specific chakra. Or breathe-in the colors of the chakras starting from the red in the root chakra to the purple in the crown chakra and breathe out any grayness out of them. You can also decorate your home or office with specific chakra colors to enhance a particular mood or attitude. These activities all heal and balance your most vital energy centers.

Why do you want to balance your chakras? These energy centers influence your being at the physical, biological and spiritual levels. Imbalances in either direction can cause illness. Sluggish chakras can cause degeneration or atrophy of organs. Overactive chakras can cause inflammation or cancer. When you work on the chakras, you clear up blocked energy in all levels and you take power back into your Self. When you reclaim your power, it is the first and most important step in lifting the veil of illusion. Furthermore, each chakra is associated with specific major organs in your physical body. Any disturbance in the subtle energy of the chakras corresponds to the organ/gland associated with that chakra. For instance, when you have a sore throat or neck pain, it is your throat chakra that is out of balance. Sit in silence, focus on that chakra, and image its color getting more and more brilliant. High blood pressure tells you the heart chakra is out of balance. High blood pressure medications will deal with the physical symptoms but do not take care of the root cause in the heart chakra. The amplitude of the heart wave is fifty times stronger than the waves of the brain, we are informed by the HearthMath Institute, and the heart's magnetic field is one thousand times stronger than that of the brain. By the time you do damage to your heart, you have depleted a significant amount of energy in that organ. You can see the critical part your heart chakra plays in your overall health.

Illness is a profound teacher. Imbalances, of which I have experienced my share, have taught me what I know about my spiritual subtle energetic body. I have had to find my own solutions as western medicine has failed me repeatedly and interventions have threatened my life. My imbalances helped me discover my deepest self by showing me how capable my body is of rejuvenating itself naturally, at times against all medical odds, and caused me to question who did I want running my belief factory. I have fired physicians from my care and they have fired me because I would not succumb to their demand to only do it their way. The latter was a grace beyond comprehension because I was forced to change the rules by which I was conditioned to live and discover a new set of internal rules and live only by my own internal voice of authority. These imbalances often were conjoined or triggered my spiritual mysticism. Illnesses may feel physical, but they are always spiritual in nature, and force you to examine the dark nights of your soul. You endure the dark nights as you become more real. Each imbalance for me has acted as a catalyst for spiritual transformation. As an energy being, I had to master reshuffling my spiritual stardust.

Through imbalances I have also learned about the incredible power of the will to heal, the incredible power of the body to heal itself if only we get out of its way. This is where consciousness plays a major role because without the knowledge of the play of the subtle chakra body and drawing on it for healing, an illness will have its way with your physical body. Imbalances have always motivated me to go further inward. They have been my blessings and my graces because they forced me to look at what diminished and/or contaminated my energy and correct it. Illnesses are your teacher and aid your spirit to become very powerful. Illnesses have developed my consciousness and taught me to depend only on Consciousness which is all there is.

Let us look at some of the connections of the chakras with your physical organs: *Crown chakra,* the highest vibrational center, is connected with the spinal cord and brain stem and pineal gland. This is your center of enlightenment and spirituality and is involved with deep inner searching. It is your center of connectedness with Source and main entry for higher energy into your physical body. Energy moves from the top down. In this chakra you dissolve into the All. As above, so below.

Brow chakra governs the eyes, pituitary and hypothalamus and pineal as well. It is located at the center of your forehead. This is associated with your intuition, clairvoyance (clear vision) and other psychic abilities. This is your "third eye" or your "inner eye" or "spiritual eye" that helps you to see within. Meditation activates the brow chakra significantly to assist you with clearer insights. On a clear day it can see into Infinity.

Throat chakra is associated with the throat, vocal cords, mouth, trachea, esophagus and bronchial tubes and thyroid gland. It also affects your general skeletal health. This is associated with speech expression, your communication and your voice center. In this chakra is where you "find your voice" and is associated with clairaudience (astral communication). Your telepathic impulses come primarily from this chakra and the glottis in back of throat.

Heart chakra governs the heart, lungs, breasts and circulatory system. It is your center of love, compassion, nurturance and empathy. The epidemic of coronary heart disease which we have in our country is linked to this chakra. Awareness of this psychoenergetic connection could help many to prevent such disorders. Although breast cancer is often associated with estrogen dominance, I have also seen many anecdotal cases in my clinical practice of women who did not feel nurtured in their lives, especially in their marriages, and were diagnosed with breast cancer. Breasts are governed by the heart chakra. Doing things from the heart center allows for miracles to occur. This is your best space for expression of love with its strongest connection to the thymus gland, in the center of the chest just below your thyroid, but in front of your heart. The thymus gland is connected to your immune system and strengthens the immune system when the thymus is activated. Do the Tarzan thump on your thymus gland and awaken and rejuvenate it as it tends to atrophy from lack of use, and from loneliness, grief or depression. We do know that it plays an important role with your immune system. Immunosuppression contributes to coronary disease in which the thymus gland plays a role. Nutrient dense foods like eggs, fish, meat activate the thymus. In the heart chakra is where you will fulfill the mandates of your human potential and is the bridge to your internal world. It is associated with clairsentience and the element of air.

Solar Plexus connects with the pancreas, liver, bladder, stomach and the large and small intestine. It is the center of your personal power and passion. It is very much linked to how you view yourself in relationships and the control and power balance of such relationships. Do you often feel powerless and victimized by others? Or do you push your own powers on others by projecting yourself on them? Do you allow *their* authenticity to come through? Is this your experience or their experience I am hearing? Am I being a genuine witness to their exchange? Each chakra has its power in its designated area. Faulty tapes being constantly replayed keep your chakras in a constant state of imbalance. The solar chakra, however, turns the power into material form. It also acts as a shield between yourself and the outside world and associated with the element of fire. When you get an energetic pressure in your solar plexus you might want to pay attention as your intuition is talking to you.

Sacral chakra oversees the bladder, prostate, ovaries, kidneys, gall bladder, bowels and spleen. It is associated with your sexuality and creativity and the element of water. This rests just below the navel area. This is your emotional chakra. Emotional turmoil resides here. It has incredible illusion-making power especially if you are overly focused on this chakra. So be attentive because if you are polarized with this chakra you can easily get into trouble by causing you to react to any impulse and view others as sexual objects. On the other hand, sexual energy can be transcended, not suppressed, into your upper chakras. This universal orgasmic force of electric–fluid currents, having established itself in an upward direction, cannot be compared to any genital stimulation or any standard sexual activity. It is unlimited and sets your entire body on fire.

Root chakra is associated with the testes, the kidneys, anus, adrenals as well as the spine. It is associated with your power of manifestation. This is your level of groundedness. How solid are your feet planted on the ground? This is your survival chakra and is associated with the element of the earth. Fear very much has its base in the root chakra. If you do not release old "garbage" you will get constipated by blocking this chakra. Or conversely you might develop diarrhea due to your dumping old "garbage" without understanding and assimilating. In the root chakra is also where the sleeping serpent lies, coiled to erupt when time is ripe. This kundalini energy is an inward flow of energy and the original source of life that when awakened ascends up the spine explodes throughout the rest of your body arousing significant spiritual energy.

This is not an exhaustive list, but it will give you a general idea of the importance of the chakra system for your healing as it connects to your various organs. Your spiritual spine, the chakras, operates at a much higher vibration than your physical spine. Therefore, if you are having a stomach ache, along with taking some intestinal restore product, meditate on the solar plexus chakra, envision yellow and watch the wheel of vortex go in a clockwise direction. Healthy chakras should spin in a clockwise direction so they can metabolize the particular energies needed from your environment. It is only when a chakra is blocked that it whirls counter-clockwise and this will slow down your basic life force. This unbalanced movement of the spin can have a profound effect on your health and indicate a serious health problem because energy is not flowing from them to your organs. They determine the state of your body and mind. Each chakra has an important lesson to teach you. When you learn to quietly listen to the message from each chakra you will be able to divert many illnesses.

You might want to balance your chakras as often as possible to keep your body healthy and feel a sense of well-being. I like to start with a few minutes of meditation before balancing the chakras. A way to balance your chakras is to sit in silence, take several deep breaths, and with each inhalation imagine your breath going from the root chakra to the crown chakra from your back. With every exhalation imagine the breath leave the crown chakra and go down to the root chakra through the front of your body. Do this up and down and circular movement of your energy several times to wake up your chakras. Relax your body by dropping those shoulders away from your ears and focus on each chakra one at a time starting with the root chakra. See it spinning clockwise as you envision it vibrantly red. To determine the spin, imagine a wall clock hanging on your chest. Then feel or visualize the direction in which the hands of the clock are moving. If you get a sense that they are moving counter-clockwise or too slowly, then stay with a particular chakra until you move the wheel clockwise and at a regular rate. Each chakra vibrates at a different speed and the vibration is faster and higher as you go up the chakra spine. The root chakra is the slowest; the crown chakra is the fastest. The size and brightness of your chakras will change and vary based on your development and based on your health. When you can balance each chakra in this way, you can heal yourself because you begin to open each chakra and release blockages. Yoga, meditation, and reiki are most effective ways to amplify and accelerate the opening of the chakras. When you practice balancing your chakras, you will prevent many diseases before you develop the need to go for pharmaceuticals. Use your multisensory perception to look inside yourself because you cannot solve your problems by using your five senses alone. Your senses keep you looking outward, and this perennial outward focus does not allow you to see the whole picture. Your multisensory abilities, on the other hand, are a direct link to your inner self.

A slightly more advanced way to balance your chakras is to do what we have already discussed but call each chakra by its seed name. These are the seed names of each of the seven chakras: Root, Muladhara is LAM; Sacral, Swadisthana is VAM; Solar Plexus, Manipura is RAM; Heart, Hridaya is YAM; Throat, Vishudha is HAM; Third Eye, Ajna is AUM; and Crown, Sahasrara is HRAUM-SAU. As you focus on each one separately, call it by its seed name and wake it up. After you do this a few times, you will learn the name of each chakra and its seed name by heart.

Still another way to balance your chakras is to stand up straight with your arms out to your sides and spin your entire body toward your right arm in a clockwise direction. This is a complete balancing exercise for the chakras. The Tibetans have recommended twenty-one spins. However, I recommend two at a time and increase slowly as your body allows. Always be near a bed or chair in case you need to sit if you get dizzy. Once you are done with your spins, raise your arms above your head and stretch your back two or three times.

Yoga is another tremendous technology for healing. Through yoga, I feel as if I touch my entire being when it is barely sunrise and I stand naked in a Sun Salutation surrendering myself to Spirit as I inhale and direct my arms into the air in an intense stretch. I bow to the earth and bring my hands to my heart in a sacred mudra gesture to balance my mind. I lie prostrate within a tangible divinity and plunge into the all-inclusive One. In yoga, I use my body to unveil my soul. Words fail me. Words are responsible for our experience of limitation. Words are responsible for our contracted condition. Cultural language has become harmful to our human process when accepted as the only way to speak about the true reality of things. My body has become my vehicle for prayer as it allows me to use my cosmic tongue with an organic, qualitative language full of symbols and poetic qualities. Spirit in action when body and consciousness become One.

Yoga forces me to live intensely and intentionally in the present moment requiring of me concentration, balance and continuous inward attention. It strengthens me because it requires me to trust my ability to sense what feels right. It cleanses me by removing the superfluous. It moves me through the Buddhist path of clear vision through right thinking and correct action. All my limbs salute the Supreme One and bow in humble reverence.

Immersed in the mystery of my body, I move my attention from the outside world, focus on the present moment, and become completely absorbed in the wilderness of my flesh. It requires of me an act of humility and receptivity as I surrender myself to the complete movement of the asana. I experience a synergistic boost as I link the various movements into a carefully chosen sequence. In yin yoga I listen to my flesh releasing stored pain, past life memories, joy, sensuality and knowledge of various kinds.

I have learned through the practice of yoga that the slightest modification of a knee or toe or finger modifies the whole asana. Just like the minutest event in life is a microcosm of the whole, every movement is the foundation upon which the next one is built. I listen intently to my feet, my palms, my throat, my uterus, my abdomen, my breasts. I walk the terrain of my body and write its autobiography as I release the flesh's inner voice through my breathing. To breathe is to feel. To limit breathing is to limit feeling. The contours of my body fade away and become enlarged beyond all measure. I pay attention to the images and feelings which arise as I move through the different parts of my body. From each part, there is a lesson to be learned. Each moment carries with it a spiritual rhythm, the contraction, the expansion, the bending, the stretching, the balancing - - they all help release the original language of the body uncontaminated by conditioning. Different, yet, all a part of the whole. It takes some effort, some stretching of the body, to get a hold of what the flesh is saying. Whenever possible, do yoga unclothe. Live in the freedom of your body.

My body is my bridge to my soul. With my body I pray. With my body I honor You oh my Great One and I bow to Thee. My whole being is in it, integrated, moving in one direction. My body and soul converge into one rhythm, one tune, and my body begins to play beautiful music. Now my mind becomes open and clear. The pace is steady and relaxed; the mood peaceful and reverent. There is a subtle flow of force that runs through my body with every position. I am animated by an Energy. I am radically alive with His Song and His Dance. I am totally relaxed with the new conception of who I AM rather than how I should be. This is a mystical path. A song surfaces from the flesh, an image, recognition of my divinity and wholeness. I embrace them without question. My body knows its rightful heritage and its rightful need. I listen to my body through my Inner Silence. It will not be deceived. "...........*You realize that all along there was something tremendous within you, and you did not know it,*" Paramahansa Yogananda.

Life is sustained from a higher frequency which expels itself into a lower frequency through sinusoidal motion from Source. As above, so below. This sinusoidal motion is the interdimensional highway of life that leads all the way to the atom from its first determinant. Therefore, the atom is the reduced equation of Infinite Creative Intelligence. The atom, your cells, your mind, and Consciousness are integrated. Another way of saying this is that Consciousness resides in each of your atoms and your mind resides in each of your cells. Consciousness is the oceanic reservoir providing the necessary nutrients for the lakes and rivers (atoms and cells) of your body. Do not nobly suffer through life as a martyr. Do something about it by understanding this energy work and crossing this bridge which is critical for your evolution because there is a better way to live!

When you concentrate on healing and aligning your chakras, your interdimensional bridge, you will be directing that higher energy through sinusoidal motion in a purposeful manner with positive intentions by being aware of your stream of electronic waveforms that are moving through you in a diametrically opposite polarity. You will no longer stay dependent on the physical. You will experience a greater sense of fullness and aliveness because you will give greater credibility to your mind rather than your brain.

I liken the brain to the computer which modulates activities between you and society. The brain is the terminal which modulates activities between Consciousness and your physical self. Your invisible Spiritual Organ (Consciousness) sustains your visible physical organs. Orthodoxy does not understand this structure but only comprehends the interrelationship of the various organs up to the brain and not beyond. It stands to reason, then, that any intervention by orthodoxy is made on incomplete information due to incomplete understanding.

TAKING FULL RESPONSIBILITY

What if when you wake up tomorrow morning, you take full responsibility for your choices. No, no, not eighty percent or ninety percent but one hundred percent responsibility for EVERTHING that comes into your awareness. What if you decided that if an experience came into your awareness, you must have a shared memory with that incident from some recent or ancestral period. I am not saying that you caused the incident, but that you do have a shared relationship in some way with everything that comes into your awareness and into your life experience – *everything!* Think of yourself playing in an orchestra. If your saxophone plays out of sequence and you do not take full responsibility for when and what you play, you will throw the entire orchestra out of its groove. Same thing with life. You have to play the music of life in total cooperation. No one instrument is more important than the other. Yet no one can play your music, only you, as you play. By taking one hundred percent responsibility you work together with the Universe.

Know that you are a composite of centuries of ancestral cells with locked in memories. We are aware of about fifteen memories at any one moment, but fifteen million memories per minute play in the background at any one time – fifteen million! We are like a computer. You may be well aware of Outlook Express, Microsoft Outlook and Windows, and Internet Explorer but to make those few programs possible and available to you, millions and millions of activities are taking place in the background outside of your awareness. This is how Consciousness works, how your mind works. What you see on Windows is comparable to your stepped down experiences of your mind into your physical self. This means that those background programs are responsible for the programs in your awareness. Whatever comes into your awareness has many background associations out of your Consciousness. Therefore, none of us really ever know what we are really doing because the fifteen million data are affecting how you receive the fifteen pieces of data into your physical self. Your present data (physical data) is downloaded and influenced from the background data (Consciousness) – like it or not. We do not see what we sense. We see what we think we sense contaminated by our conditioned trash. What you experience directly is an illusion contaminated by your ancestral memories. You are also really always experiencing life one-half second behind your unconscious memory.

If you believe that you are a wave in one sea of consciousness, then that wave shares the properties, the "memories", of the ocean. When we separate the wave from the ocean the properties remain the same. Therefore, you [the wave] share memories with every human being [the ocean] that exists or has existed. In other words, if you keep building trash upon trash cleansing is critical and essential. You need to cleanse memories that have created the build-up in order to get back to your core, your Divinity.

So how do you cleanse: By saying to Divinity within you [not to the person in front of you or to anyone else outside of you] *I am sorry, please forgive me, I love you, and thank* you as suggested by Dr. Hui Len in his book, <u>Zero Limits</u>, on the Hawaiian spiritual ritual of Ho'oponopono. Every time you repeat these cleansing phrases you peel a leaf from the artichoke until you finally get to the heart of the artichoke – the core of your Divinity. You peel the layer of the onion until you get to the nothingness of the onion.

Your role in life is singular – to reach your Divinity. Cleansing aids you in reaching this Divinity. When you reach this state, Everything is available. Once you get rid of the trash, you will receive inspiration. You reach your Divinity by constant cleansing – all day long. Thank the chair you sit on and tell it you love it. Thank and love your computer. Thank and love the food you eat. Thank your car when you get in it – every time. Thank and love every person, animal or thing that comes into your awareness. This and every moment matters. Everything is alive.

We are all electromagnetic energy only at different evolutionary stages. Everything wants to know it is loved and thanked no matter what its evolutionary stage however. Every time you say the cleansing words you will be cleansing your accumulated dirt. Everything is really an opportunity about you – an opportunity to cleanse. Once you start to cleanse, you will never return to your previous state as miracles begin to happen right in front of your eyes daily. Thank you and I love you. As above, so below. Become speechless and discover your inner Self. You must develop a spiritual partnership with yourself before you develop a spiritual partnership with anybody else. Creating authentic power begins with you.

Do not settle for a contracted limited printout from your computer brain. You have other templates in your Mind Computer which you can download besides the one you see on your computer screen. The mind is not your brain. Your mind is cyberspace which provides a multitude of choices; your brain is reflected in your contracted computer screen. Do you like what you see on your personal life computer screen?

Just as your computer has a limited life which does not affect cyberspace once the computer stops functioning, so does your brain have a limited life, which does not affect Consciousness/Mind. Your brain, like the computer, is perishable. Your mind is imperishable. Become wise and wake up to this logic. Yet, I myself am only one drop of water, how can I explain to you the Ocean? My words feel insufficient.

Your subtle body is your primary body and must be the focus of treatment for permanent healing. You could not exist without your subtle body. Become intimately informed and connected with your subtle body. Awaken to the unseen forces within your life and within your body. We are obsessed with technological progress, but do not realize that the most efficient and powerful technology lies within each one of us. By becoming attuned to this inner technology, you will prevent many illnesses by circumventing diseases early on in their progression. Energy is the magnificent dance of the medium of your Spirit which the ancient masters and sages have taught for many centuries. Chakra work, reiki and meditation, yoga and cleansing are ways to extend the boundary lines from the physical to the subtle, the identity of your true origin. If you do not do this work, you will calcify precious energy into your physical anatomy.

QUANTUM REIKI AS A
SPIRITUAL TECHNOLOGY

Reiki

Reiki is a multidimensional energy and spiritual technology for global change. It is about being open to the energy from Source that comes through the palms of your hands. It is like your computer or phone, it works for everyone. Even though some people do not have a clue how some technology works, it will still work for anyone who is willing to take the time to learn. I am very elementary and rudimentary in the use of a computer. Yet, computer technology is very sophisticated. I could do a lot more with a computer if I were interested in doing so. Reiki is the same. You can use it a little or you can exploit all its unlimited possibilities for realizing your ultimate nature and end goals. It is the technology for using your energies for higher possibilities and for healing yourself and facilitating healing for others. This ability to sense energies is available to all of us and not just a select few. We are all multidimensional with multisensory abilities. You learn to detect qualitative changes and irregularities in your body or the body of another locally or remotely. The target does not matter. Energy works the same. With reiki you break the limitations of this encapsulated physical dimension. If you continue to receive your reference point from the third dimension, you will continue to live your life with limitations. To believe in your limitations is a spiritual aneurysm that blocks your further growth. When you finally realize that you are a fourth dimensional being, you open the aperture to the window of your soul. You can only regenerate when you realize that you have support from a higher dimensional energy field. A client recently asked me, "How is it that you can detect such energies in people's bodies and I cannot?" I responded, "I *know* who I AM and you do not!" I am not special. We all have this remarkable capability of these sensory experiences through the palms of our hands for exchange of energy. A warm touch is a powerful tool and should not be underestimated. I am awake to our multidimensional reality and make use of its biofield. You have to find your way by practicing energy activities. Personally, subtle energy and human experience take precedence over science, and one day we shall see the eccentricity of science.

Quantum physics clearly supports the work of reiki. We have discussed throughout this book that we are vibratory energy beings made up of the building blocks of atoms which are made up of electrons, protons and neutrons. These particles are translated into positive or negative energy waves of specific frequencies and vibrations. Stronger vibrations will take over weaker vibrations science has proven and informed us through quantum physics. Therefore, a strong healthy practitioner channeling reiki through her hands will take over the weaker particles of a weakened recipient to match practitioner's stronger vibrations activating a stronger healing potential. This ability for stronger vibrations taking over weaker vibrations explains the science and principles behind reiki. Reiki has followed quantum physics way before we have had any evidence provided to us by science. These waves also follow the physical phenomenon of quantum entanglement principles because the particles of both individuals, practitioner and healee, become linked together and influence one another, whether in close proximity or at a distance, since we work in a nonlinear and nonlocal environment in reiki. This quantum entanglement is at the heart of disparity between western medicine and quantum medicine as it violates classical linear and local realism.

Dr. Masaru Emoto, a Japanese scientist, businessman and author, demonstrated numerous times in his research how the electromagnetic field coming from a person's words affected the molecular makeup of water. Your body is seventy-five percent water. Through intention you can change this environment within your body that then creates an effect on your cellular structure. We know that every cell, every organ, and every body has its own vibration, and this is affected by the intention in reiki. Cells communicate through the music that they emit. The harmony of this sound changes when a cell goes out of balance. What you say and do during reiki will have a measurable influence on the cells of your target and will influence the blood of your target as well whether it is you or someone else, whether it is local or remote healing. Energy is spaceless so it does not matter whether the target you are healing is in the same room with you or two thousand miles away. Energy is energy. It knows no distance. Intentional healing is epigenetics at its very best since we know that environment affects genetic expression. Your intention can alter the heritable trait in gene expression. Through the intention of reiki, you can change the molecular structure, chemistry and pH balance of your body without relying on pharmaceuticals nor machines, as subjects, repeatedly and successfully, changed the molecular structure of water in Emoto's research clearly delineated in his 2004 New York Times best seller book the Hidden Messages in Water.

The hands-on healing that comes through the palms of your hands through Source is a doorway into a world of greater control over your health because you learn to shift the energies in your body. The reiki kanji symbol itself means the life force of Universal Wisdom. The top half of the symbol, rei, is Universal Wisdom and the bottom half, ki, is life force. Reiki revitalizes mind, body and spirit. In reiki you become a Source technician, an intermediary, and make the "impossible" possible and the intangible tangible since we are all plugged into the same field of Consciousness. Your realization in reiki that you are plugged into the same pattern as the larger field will bring about a statistical similarity in the electromagnetic field which we call coherence. You join two minds together through the quantum field. This entanglement is an ideal situation for healing. You turn fiction into reality because you reach into the world of probability and make them your reality. Reiki helps you to keep your energies vital, strong and harmonious. It offers you an ancient source of power, hopefulness and inspiration for transforming yourself and the world around you, since peace grows outward from enlightened individuals. As you do reiki, you will notice a greater intuitive awareness and sensitivity as long as you come from a heart that is simple and sincere. Reiki is a process much larger than ourselves.

Reiki is about being a channel for Divine energy. It is an energy practice that involves channeling and delivering Universal Life energy from Source because you are the human expression of Source. In reiki you become the conduit for Source between you and a client. Through reiki practice you become a true channel, by balancing your own mind and body (spiritual and material aspects), and you will open your own self to a much higher vibration. You will then begin to change the molecular and cellular structure of your own body as you treat yourself with reiki or treat another. I perform reiki with myself every morning during the hours of 4:30 a.m. and 6:30 a.m. With every treatment, I know I bring more light into my own cells and realign my chakras.

The reiki system of hands-on healing draws on the chakras as well as specific symbols and mantras to connect you with Source. These symbols and mantras are the keys to opening the doors to a higher consciousness. They also aid in triggering an intention for healing. Because in reiki you are communicating your being not a technique, it is critical that you do your own work before administering reiki to anybody else besides yourself. Reiki practice, however, will increase your spiritual awareness and growth and your connection to Source. It will most definitely help you to develop your intuition and to listen to your inner voice. You do reiki through guidance and inspiration. Practice, practice, practice, as often as possible. I have been training others in reiki remotely and globally for years in six out of seven continents. Furthermore, when I have an injury or an imbalance of any sort, I do self-reiki two to three times daily. The more you perform reiki the more you feel the energy in the palms of your hands.

When you have the intention to experience energy and information, this connects you not only with yourself or with another but also with Source. It is this dynamic connection that organizes, controls, self-regulates and brings order. This energy exchange between two systems is called resonance. The two systems become a point of reference for one another as in quantum entanglement. The waves of energy coming from Source will travel into your body, the receiver, and find resonance with your energy system bringing it into balance. There is a tendency for the slower vibration body, that of your client, to synchronize and attempt to match the body of higher vibration, that of the Reiki Master.

Furthermore, we have significant research showing the enzymatic action that takes place with hands-on-healing such as reiki. Reiki can repair damaged enzymes, cellular workhorses that speed up metabolic reactions, through the energetic effect of this spiritual technology. Enzymes, biological catalysts, lower the amount of energy needed for reactions to progress in the cells. Hands-on-healing techniques, therefore, such as reiki can affect the enzyme kinetic expression, reintegrate and structurally reorganize damaged enzymes and decrease entropy. This activity then results in greater cellular health. Reiki, therefore, provides a very much needed energy boost to assist a patient achieve balance. One can see how reiki is negatively entropic in its basic nature.

As a reiki practitioner, therefore, you are able to induce measurable healing benefits in yourself or another person. Would not this be an exceptional skill to be taught to physicians and all other medical professionals to amplify their existing medical abilities. It should not be one over the other, but a marriage of quantum medicine and allopathic care.

A further bioenergetic change that has been observed is an increase in hemoglobin values through hands–on–healing. Hemoglobin is the iron–rich protein found in red blood cells. This bioenergetic change in hemoglobin is very similar to the chlorophyll increase we see when we do reiki with plants. These are measurable results that indicate reliable physiological changes through reiki. We have many biochemical yardsticks to measure the activity induced internally between the healer and the healee through reiki.

We have discussed earlier the spinal chakras in <u>The Quantum Life</u>. However, the palms of the hands also have two minor chakras which act as centers of energy and the reiki healer transfers this energy to the healee through the palms of the hands. Hence, the reason the healer rubs his hands together before a treatment in order to bring to the surface rapidly this energy in the palm chakras. These chakras act as a transient energy link between the two individuals very similar to quantum entanglement. These changes are induced by first attuning oneself through meditation and then laying–on–of–hands to act as conduits for a higher Source of energy. As a reiki healer you have measurable energy effects in retarding the formation of certain diseases by altering the chemistry of the body. We have also seen very rapid wound healing as a result of treatment with reiki. We have seen the molecular make–up of water change through reiki which then can be consumed by a healee for healing benefits. As a reiki healer you can affect the cellular expression of many disease states through the magnetic fields produced in the hands, a magnetic field much greater than that of the earth's magnetic field. This is a magnetic field of significant intensity. The longer you hold your hands over a healee, the more rapid the reaction rate. Furthermore, the vibrational frequency which the healer brings to the table will determine the level at which healing will occur. Disease is multidimensional and must be healed at a multidimensional level and not just the physical. Reiki is the vehicle for such healing.

You were born with this ability to heal yourself and facilitate the healing of others. It is a skill that also can be taught. Do not let anyone tell you differently. It is your birthright to be in direct connection with Infinite Creative Intelligence, the One Source. I am only re-awakening you to restructuring the energy from your chakras, meditation and reiki and sending it out of your hands for your benefit and the benefit of others. Keep it simple.

You never know what will come up in reiki. When treating others, I have been able to access sexual abuse, abortions, cancer and various other disorders in the body that were causing great disharmony. Specifically, one client was sent to me by her oncologist because of repeated cervical/uterine cancer. In reiki treatment I picked up imbalances in that area that were informed to me through my hands and through Source as being potential promiscuity/abortion. During the debriefing as I mentioned my findings, she sobbed profusely, uttering that no one, not even the oncologist nor her husband knew of this abortion. The "secret" blocked her energy in her female organs as she never cleared them by keeping the secret confined.

Another client's body expressed significant vibration during reiki around the pelvic area. My hands through Source informed me of sexual abuse in her childhood. In the debriefing she admitted to years of sexual abuse by a brother.

An additional client was sent to me by his Internist for "psychosomatic" disorder. Under reiki I was able to detect that he may need to be examined by an Oncologist. I picked up imbalances around his spleen. I recommended such an exam, and he dismissed it relating that he has been in and out of doctor's offices for the last year, been examined by some of the best doctors in the country since his wife was also a physician, and these physicians all suggested it was psychosomatic and sent him to me for therapy. I urged him to consider another exam by someone nonlocal such as Mayo or Cleveland Clinics. I expressed to him I disagreed with the psychosomatic diagnosis from his medical team. The following week he did not show up for his appointment, very much uncharacteristic of this very responsible man. I called to check on him at home and when no one answered the phone, I called his employer asking for him very casually. His employer told me he had died the day before from cancer in his spleen.

I have had several reiki treatments myself. I have burst into laughter in reiki, and I have burst into tears during reiki. Other times I laid there peacefully. At times during reiki my body went into overmode vibrations. The most remarkable treatment I had was by Dr. Lawr, M. D. and his wife. I had three sessions with this reiki team but the third one was unusual.

In my other two reiki sessions with the Lawr team, I left feeling joyful. In the third session I left full of sadness. Fifteen minutes into our ride home, I started with a headache which did not remit for hours later. I felt as if I was going through a detoxification process. When my husband and I arrived home, I found the need to lay down on the couch. I felt very tired, inwardly focused, and increasingly sad. I laid on the couch half-awake half asleep until 5:30 p.m. I eventually got up off the couch, ate some light supper, only to feel the need to lay back down until 9 p.m. again. This was very uncharacteristic of me, and I wondered what was brewing. I could not seem to pick up my energy. I went to bed that evening, slept all night but still awakened with remarkable sadness.

In the morning around 8:45 a.m., I was walking down to our lower level to start a load of laundry, and the words came suddenly and unexpectedly rolling in my mind, *"I can see clearly now."* This repeated about ten times rapidly as I walked down the steps, and then my full awareness went to the sudden sensation of significant pressure on my abdomen. I had felt this same sensation in my abdomen in the reiki session as if the practitioners' hands were on my abdomen pressing with a ton of brick. I do not know if the practitioners were actually pushing or if it only felt that way as stored memories were surfacing. I remember thinking, "oh my, they have their full weight on my body." After this sensation on my abdomen that I was feeling in the morning, and as I walked down the steps with intense energy flowing and pushing down vaginally, the realization was loudly clear to the ears of my soul, *"Oh my gosh, I lost a child!"* At this point I sobbed profusely, wailed, rolled like a fetus for a half hour seeing images of a third trimester baby boy being born to me, placed in my arms, took one breath, and baby transitioned!"

I asked the spirit of the child what he needed that he is coming to me at this time and in this way. He said, *"I needed you to know me, I needed you to see me clearly. I needed you to call my name just once."* At this point I said through my tears, *"Nicholas I love you; you may go now and finish your journey."* He left whispering to me, *"Mama, I am watching over you. I am always with you. I love you."* He left and so did the sadness.

This is the third child *every* psychic, without exception, has picked up when they have done a reading with me. Although Nicholas was not a child of this lifetime, he had been trying to make himself visible to me in this lifetime through many sources for several decades. It is Nicholas's lingering energy around me that the psychics were picking up each time they would tell me that I had three children in this lifetime. I would correct them by informing them that I have only two children and did not have any miscarriages. They would always look confused. I would feel the same confusion because this revelation was consistent. Once Nicholas came through as a result of this reiki session, no psychic or medium has since picked up a third child energy around me.

When you have these experiences, you may be doubtful about their reliability because you do not understand yourself. I am filled with peace and light after such epiphanies and visions, and I feel internally assured they come only from Infinite Intelligence. Furthermore, the more of these experiences I have, the more humble I become. They all happen for me spontaneously and without anticipation nor expectations. I cannot stop these experiences of my soul being suspended in such rapture that draw me out of my senses once they start, any more than I can make the sun stop shining. They are so impressed in my memory that I never forget them. They are unexplainable, but never forgotten. They always increase my desire to further align and be reabsorbed in Source. I experience these mystical experiences not with my vision but with my soul. They all have added a deeper interior enlightenment. I walk with confidence in knowing that I AM that I AM. Do not be timid any longer. Take all the favors you are given. Walk in your divinity.

VISIONS OF THE NIGHT

Dreams are another portal to another reality, a dimension of unlimited possibilities, through which visions and intuitions communicate with you. They are powerful agents for change and inform you that you are so much more than what you think you are. The unlimited and collective wisdom and visions which come from dreams are within the reach of everyone. Dreams are a timeless source of guidance, wisdom and learning when you use them properly. Journal them because they are easily lost upon waking.

Transitional states between sleeping and waking are extraordinarily fruitful times for your dreams. I recall one morning, as I was in the hypnagogic state, a state of intermediate consciousness, a state of half-asleep and half-awake which we often experience before fully waking in the morning, I heard a knock on our front door. I opened the door and a uniformed trooper informed me that my husband was riding in a pickup truck coming from Ellsworth, a nearby town, and the driver had been drinking, hit a semi-truck and the driver was killed. My husband, the passenger, was in intensive care and in critical condition at the hospital. I sobbed so profusely that I awakened myself from the dream.

I could not stop weeping as I showered and dressed to go to my clinic that morning to begin a full day of seeing patients. Before I left, however, I noticed a note from my husband requesting that I drop over a document to him since I passed him on my way to my own office. As I met my husband, I was still weeping. I could not seem to stop. Puzzled to see me in this state he questioned, *"What is the matter, I have never seen you this way?"* I related to him the dream, and as I mentioned the rural town of Ellsworth, a town which we rarely have reason to visit, *his* face turned white. Noting the sudden change in him I asked, *"What is the matter with YOU, you have turned pale."*

He took a deep breath and informed, *"I have a meeting in Ellsworth this evening and I am being picked up in a pickup truck by Ben."*

It is important to stay focused on the mystery of dreams. This precognitive dream was a vehicle through which my intuition made itself known. My husband changed his plans. This precognitive dream may very well have saved his life and the life of the driver. Precognitive dreams are a way that we reach into the vast inner space of our eternal nonlocal mind as Larry Dossey, M.D., physician and author of *Recovering The Soul*, instructs. Dr. Dossey lectures globally about the importance of consciousness and spirituality in medicine. Dreams are a source of inner knowledge. The wisdom and power of dream experience can transform your life.

Intuition flows freely during dreamtime, because your dreams are uncensored. Intuition does not always supply the right answers, but it always supplies the right questions which will guide you to the right answer. Intuition is the thought which comes to a person instantly in any situation before a person has time to think and reason. It is that thug in your solar plexus, your third chakra. Trusting and living through your intuition, your sixth sense, will move you to become a person who wants to develop the larger Self. The goal, although important, is not as important as the journey.

One of our first astronauts, Edgar Mitchell, had a peak experience, as we discussed earlier, which gave him the confidence to begin living through his movement. It gave him the grounding to move within the journey itself. The journey is everything and it demands being mindful of the sacredness of the present moment. Astronaut Edgar Mitchell honored his sixth sense during the Apollo 14 flight. He was spiritually transformed while in the command module on the basis of what he was seeing out of the cockpit window while viewing the earth.

Edgar Mitchell has now transitioned, but before transitioning he founded the Noetic Science Institute whose mission has been to research and support psychical reality which is as real or more real than physical reality. How Edgar Mitchell viewed and embraced his experience during the Apollo 14 flight has directly affected his spiritual growth and his life intention. It has transformed him for a force for good. His own transformation and trust in his inner being has since transformed millions of others on planet earth.

When you begin to believe that the crises life generates are opportunities for spiritual emergence, and not necessarily an emergency, and depend for direction on your sixth sense, your intuition or your dreamtime, you will ask different questions and take different answers than you would ordinarily. In making this integral shift, in perception, from being acted upon by life to becoming actively involved in the process of living, you will develop a consciousness of choice which will enhance your life on every level.

IMMORTALITY THROUGH MORPHOGENESIS

The more you heighten your awareness of the interdimensional nature of your life, the more selective you can become in directing positive, rather than negative, energy through the interdimensional highway of your life. The more you are aware of the continuity of your thoughts, the more you can control the energy that comes with the polarity factors (positive/negative). I will not be so foolishly audacious as to say I understand fully all these Truths because Truth is an infinite perspectus. I live them and feel them, but words fail me to explain them to your satisfaction. Start searching them out for yourself. Do not take my word for it. I remember when I was in the psychology clinical program, one of my professors had a poster hanging on his wall whose words I have never forgotten: "Humility is seeing yourself as you truly are." What I am is one in constant and earnest search for the Truth. Beyond that I know very little.

My words fall short because so many of the experiences are unexplainable. How can words ever express the ultimate Truth. Yet the experiences leave an indelible mark from which my knowing comes. It reminds me of the Zen phrase, "The minute you begin to speak about a thing, you miss the mark!" Therefore, I concentrate solely on the experiences rather than their interpretation. Radical empiricism I suppose one might say. When you find out for yourself, you will be left with no doubts. Watch, don't think. Just look inside yourself. Observe. Listen in Silence. Shift awareness from the rational to the intuitive mode of Consciousness.

Rational and logical reasoning in orthodoxy and the western model have always been their main tools. They certainly have their utility and legitimate function but not in the search for Truth because logic and rationalism make people intolerant and finite in their positions. It is valuable but insufficient. The Quantum Life through quantum energy/medicine/spirituality, on the other hand, is not afraid to go beyond this logic because we know through quantum physics that reality transcends rational and logical reasoning and believes in your inherent harmony and infinity. Infinity is not logical as it is always changing and transforming. In this transcendence ordinary language often fails us and has failed us with our present evolutionary crisis. It is responsible for significant accomplishments in the external world with monstrous commercialism but has not succeeded in any issues of the heart and soul. Increased knowledge; decreased heart.

The Quantum Life knows we have no meaning as isolated entities. It supports and instructs us about our Oneness. If there is an imbalance in the way of the Tao or the blended harmony of the yin and yang you encounter a spiritual and medical illness. It continuously imparts to you that you are nothing in yourself and the idea of a separate self is an illusion. Quantum's most important characteristic is mutual interrelatedness. We are all an integrated part of the Whole. No matter what happens to you externally, you remain anchored internally in this Wholeness. It is this Wholeness toward which we must strive to uncover again because we are too imperfect in our material self. We are a dynamic inseparable whole.

Consciousness can never be fully comprehended. Yet transformation and change are essential to our progressive evolution. You mature through this constant flow of transformation and change by trusting your intuitive intelligence which is innate in you. Your consciousness is going to be pitched information from many sources of opposing polarities. However, you will be capable of interpreting the nature of this information the more you expand your awareness rather than your own self-interest or lofty perch. Reiki, meditation, and chakra work are a diagrammatic schematic for your progressive evolution. If you do not increase, you will decrease.

With a Force of Consciousness, there is no reason why we cannot expect and strive for immortality such as Babaji, a scholar who spoke several languages. I cannot think of one reason why immortality would not be possible. Mahatavar Babaji manifested himself before

Jesus and mentored Jesus and Kabir. He has never dropped his body and lives in the caves of the Himalayan Mountains with several other Spiritual Masters. Every particle of Babaji's being is filled with God-Consciousness. Many other Masters have experienced Babaji directly and written about him. He conquered death at age 16 and his body has not aged beyond that point. He has attained a supreme state of enlightenment. He instructs through silence. He is Absolute Existence. He went from a soul carrying corpse to concentrated energy which obeys his will. He is selfless, humorous and filled with humility. I have been graced with his "presence" through a medium as an intermediary. Knowing now that I create my world, I can easily say that I drew him to myself through the medium because I am ready for his energy in my life. I never feel alone with Babaji overshadowing me, and I am often guided telepathically by Babaji. I channel him for moment-to-moment discussions for greater clarity. My soul's incessant desire is that one day soon he will grace me with his visual presence directly. Om Kriya Babaji Nama Aum (Guru, God and Self are ONE). As you move forward in your evolution link up with your "spiritual" teacher, physical or non-physical, by invoking his or her name. It is a wonderful support system.

The archetype for immortality has been set and according to the morphogenetic field theory of Rupert Sheldrake, this influence can facilitate itself because of the collective memory. Once a precedent has been set, it is more likely to occur again as it becomes available through a wave of possibilities into the material form. If you can conceive it, you can create it. Immortality, however, must be done organically and spiritually and not through artificial intelligence to create synthetic beings with false power.

Morphogenesis is the next pathway to our spiritual evolution. Remember that m-fields are nonlinear, spaceless and timeless and maintain the integrity of the original form and its probabilistic organizing abilities. So why should m-fields not be an aid for our next step in our greater evolution. We know we are illimitable. We are slowed-down Light. With a change in consciousness, we shall discover the means and energy of immortality. I know we can emerge a greater status and have our higher Consciousness descend permanently into our physical and lower self. But first we must permanently ascend from the slow lower vibration of the lower to higher, and then back down from higher to our lower nature which will become saturated with waves of Infinite knowledge for our immortality. Here all will unfold its powers. This will be pure perfection.

We need to collectively share this vision of change and make a gigantic inner leap in consciousness. Get in the driver's seat by letting it percolate and manifest in your Silence first. Then master it. According to the m-fields, these experiences repeat themselves until they become normal. Mahatavar Babaji has already created the prototype as he lives a Divine life on earth. The blueprint for our immortality is already available. Let us download it by listening to inspirations and intuitions or a greater insight, which will begin to get rid of all our confusions and doubts, and a new consciousness will emerge. Trust your intuition. It is a revealing flash of a superior light. Turn your consciousness inward. Live from within. This will bring an enlargement. When there is an inner opening, new powers of consciousness will develop in you. You will create your purpose as you advance. There is nothing irrational about this. I see it as a natural, organic, and necessary next step in our formulations from spiritual beings to superbeings. It is spiritual completeness of life itself.

There is no limit to this revolution. Your expectation will influence your outcome. You will be invaded by Spirit! Your immortality will then go from a belief to pure self-awareness of all that you are and all the unbounded largeness that you can be. Start calling on the supramental. Start sharing the belief and planting the seed in others of our organic immortality, so we can get it into the collective. Babaji has forged the path. Let us follow.

THERE IS A BETTER WAY TO LIVE

If only you could see your face through my eyes
you would realize how beautiful you are....
Rumi

This book is an outpouring of my heart and soul. My deepest hope is that your limitations will melt away in the awakened and blissful awareness of Consciousness, the sole reality. Through practical guidance and intimate stories, I hope to have conveyed that Consciousness is the permanent solution to life's enduring problems. The Quantum Life will provide you passion, heart and soul and birth you as a spiritual seeker.

The Quantum Life is a doorway. It is up to you if you want to reach for the door knob. Once you go through the doorway, you will begin to see with different eyes and ask different questions. Some questions are best answered in silence. The novelty of silence is infinite in its profundity of insight and newness of ideas. In this silence you can continue indefinitely to uncover new truths. These truths will not originate in the brain but from a subtle mechanism outside space and time and are transferred superluminally. These truths will often culminate in a quantum leap beyond rationality. This is the road to your enlightenment.

If you like what you read in this book, consider that it came from Source, Infinite Intelligence. If there are parts you do not like, consider that they came from me, from my dullness, in my sincere attempt to provide you the *cognitive world* of infinity by which I have been swallowed. I no longer find the smallest value in meeting the external needs of a "system". Hopefully, after reading this book on the psychology of consciousness, you cannot possibly be content with remaining the same. Furthermore, it is my hope that you have started to overcome the most formidable of all diseases, ignorance. <u>The Quantum Life</u> provides you armor against this disease. At minimum it has awakened your awareness in seeing that the external world is very confused. It is therefore imperative that you do not mistake the shadows on the wall for the real world.

Self-realization through the quantum life is not a state you have to attain but realized because it is within you from the very beginning. If you set your heart on finite and material goals and continue to cling frantically on floating logs, you will always be disappointed and it will leave you in a hopeless and impossible state. I guarantee you that the material alone will lead you to a blind alley. You will forget to behave like God. Be less concerned with exterior activities and appearances but focus on your own inner character. Penetrate beneath the external surface of your life and get beyond orthodoxy. Do not rest content beyond anything but your own divine essence. Access your divine essence through the quantum life. Live only in the Eternal Now in loving embrace with our Creative Artist, an infinity of inexhaustible life.

Infinite Intelligence leads each one of us as It sees necessary. The path delineated in <u>The Quantum Life</u> is a preparation for becoming a very good servant of Consciousness. You decide how you want to use your power. What is worth much, costs much. As you begin, you will awaken others. Find your voice so that your silence is not a lie. What I hope to have achieved in this book to some extent is to have provided you organic experiences that have given my life meaning and joy and have the potential to do the same for you if only you are receptive. Knowledge is transformative. Most of these experiences have emerged from a meditative state of consciousness. The organic view of life is supported by quantum physics and is more fundamental than the mechanistic Newtonian physics.

<u>The Quantum Life</u> is not a trend. <u>The Quantum Life</u> is a Movement. <u>The Quantum Life</u> is an archetypal organization for soul survival through the study of the regenerative principles of progressive evolution. It is a deep analysis of how you have become ill and provides you advanced psychotherapeutic tools to heal yourself.

It instructs how all life needs to be lived in the spirit because your beliefs influence your actions. Do you want your life to be defined solely by your paycheck and social life? This is your life and no one life is a mere dress rehearsal. Then The Quantum Life is your solution because it provides you the longest vision in the room!

As you educate yourself through The Quantum Life you will weaken the hold of orthodoxy as it shows you a deeper and different reality behind the superficial and mechanistic phenomenon which you see in everyday life. Perhaps a synthesis and mutual influence between physics and mysticism can serve the planet well. At this point, I hope you have become aware of the essential nature of the unity of all things, and that you are an integral part of this Oneness. There are many nonlocal instantaneous variables that connect you to this Oneness. Everything manifests from this Oneness.

Journey into this Infinity in full consciousness of the regenerative principles of life. Investigate for yourself. You can only know who you are through personal experience. Without Consciousness you are dead. Everything is Consciousness. The formless Consciousness is Infinite. You cannot set out to obtain it. You need to uncover it from your silence. Do not worship your silence, however; worship only that which leads from your Silence.

Consciousness is what you are. However, consciousness, which is connected to your human form, is time-bound and limited. At some point your physical consciousness will just simply leave. Since it is energy, it will be transformed and fuse and merge into Consciousness.

Come with me to that inner place. Do not go back to your ordinary consciousness. Rather go to that place beyond time and space. Together let us make a difference. Let us heal the soul of this planet. Meditate and draw others to this path of the quantum life. Through The Quantum Life I have jump-started your learning of transcending the perpetual motion picture of illusions by encouraging you to look into your mental and spiritual account book to find out what has eaten up the profits of your soul's joy. The Quantum Life has jump-started the battery of your inner power. Now it is up to you to keep your vehicle operational by mandating a strong personal responsibility and integrity toward your progressive evolution.

What were you before your form came into being? Consciousness! This is your root. No longer stray to the leaves and the branches. Your present state of affairs is ephemeral and transient. Once you remove all the adulterations of your conditioned upbringing, you will know that God is you. You are the absence of the phenomenon of your human form, that which you see. Your soul is a speck of immortal substance encapsulated in the shell of your physical body. Together let us feed the soul and do it organically and spiritually.

Stop living a robot-like existence by stepping back a bit. Stabilize in your true identity by first stepping into more allowing. Seek truths that are not connections to social and cultural norms. In any situation, tune into it with full awareness to determine how much it resonates with your heart. This process takes patience as this ripple keeps coming and going. Wait. See. *You* are what you are seeking. The "System" will utilize you in the area of your strength. I am strong in the mental and the spiritual. I write books and teach to inspire others to see the sacredness in the ordinary. Someone else may be strong in the physical and the "System" will utilize that individual in that capacity to inspire others through their unique calling.

If you have reached this point in the book, then you have started your "homework" in the gallery of your mind because it creates a certain motion of consciousness. It means you are up and have awakened from your somnambulism. Life will now begin to respond to you in a fuller sense as you grow in your security that comes in recognizing that all is within *you* and you are experiencing what you are manifesting. Infuse your passion and purpose and follow your own unique journey. No longer live someone else's life.

Transformational processes can cause discomfort. Do not overreact. They are all stepping stones. This is your entry point. Keep stretching yourself as I have continued to stretch myself by the writing of this book. The writing of this book has awakened an even deeper relationship to my own energy and Earth energies in a way that it had never flowed before. Through this stretching, we reframe ourselves, we change, and we grow. The brain has tremendous neuroplasticity. By beginning to think differently we begin to change neuropathways. Have self-determination and choose who you are.

From reading this book, you will reach levels of understanding you couldn't reach before. From there you need to create a consensus reality and share this focus with others so that others can assume this movement with you. You now have the archetype of a quantum life. Bring in co-creators. Educate the educators. I have done my part in bringing you in as a co-creator toward the quantum life by writing this book and making it available for you to read. Do yours to energize that part now because co-creation helps to not burn out our system. We can only do this together. Think of these co-creators as our Source neighbors. Do not go back out of your Sourceness. Think only in terms of Oneness. Seek out the energy and spiritual meaning of every situation you encounter. Breathe Source into your being every second of your life. A young friend recently said to me, "My father has really challenged me. He requires a lot of forgiveness, and I am still growing in that area." I responded, "No, your dad requires no forgiveness. We are the ones requiring the forgiveness for being judgmental. We have yet to learn to behave like God."

Luxuriate in your Beingness. Stay grounded. Look at life with fresh eyes. Throw out the oppression that has conditioned you all your life. What you know now is the foundation for your next step. Keep energizing it by spreading the archetype. Ignite others into appreciation of their own Consciousness. Together now we must stimulate the process by helping more people to tune into themselves and get their teachings from within. No single raindrop is ever responsible for the flood. We need to do this together. Your fifth chakra will compel you to express all that you have learned about the quantum life.

What are you going to make of your life as a quantum being? Perhaps choose spirit rather than your present illusory life. What will you do as a more awakened human being in this world? Perhaps invest more of yourself in your internal power. Are you willing and able psychologically to develop a different way of living by continuing to take an interest in external activities of life at the same time that you make a radical change internally psychologically and spiritually? Perhaps limit the authority of the material world and opt more for your inner world.

Change is possible in increments and over a period of time. It takes time to reconstruct your life little by little. However, change is also possible instantly. We are capable of quantum leaps overnight if you want a wider, deeper, more extensive vision. With this quantum leap do not expect to behave in some unusual way, nor should you, or appear or be totally different than the ordinary person. You will still go about normally; yet you will be filled with bliss, purity and peace because you will have realized the Truth. It is inside of you that the changes will take place as you take part in the cosmic Game of the Life Divine. Face your Infinity without flinching but rather with serenity.

Through your progressive development, you will be connecting more with what is happening now, but you will often still be reacting on what had been. This is the beginning of your understanding. It is a gradual unfoldment. It takes a while to integrate all this. You will keep seeding your learning into a greater potential. It is going to change the way you look at everything. Knowing is not enough, however, you must apply what you are learning.

Stop being mentally lethargic about your evolution. You are in the womb of Source and you are emerging. There is no rush because the one constant is eternity. Yet that boredom and that discontent are your divinity crying to come to the forefront. Serve your divinity with all that you are and all that you have. Serve your divinity by becoming one with your Consciousness so that you will expand into the infinite expanse of the Divine Ocean. There is only one reality, Consciousness. Everything evolves from Consciousness. Consciousness is the only foundation. That is the Law of Spirit. Die to your present self and become that which you want the most. Forget what was. Press toward hitting the mark. Incarnate your new self by imagining that you already are that which you most want to be because you already have within you that which you are seeking. Persist. Live in this spirit of confidence. Have unending determination in your conviction that I AM that!

Your most sublime achievement on the earth plane can only come from the inner plane of your Consciousness because the most powerful technology in the world is your Consciousness. Your earthly accomplishments will be reflections of your inner activities and developments. Wherever you place your awareness is where your energy goes. The physical world with which you have surrounded yourself is a product of your Consciousness. May your consciousness embrace the universe, and may your speech only express the Truth. There is only Consciousness.

I am encouraging you to live at a higher level of consciousness and to honor your own inner experience because the world wants to absorb you. The Quantum Life is a reliable map for the journey of your soul. Cherish what calls out to you whether valued by culture, because orthodox culture is a pale shadow of a deeper order. Your Consciousness is the true symphony of life, the true spiritual dance of life. Dance often and well. Consciousness cuts across time periods so that following fads is a great way to get outdated. When you marry the spirit of the time through orthodoxy, you will soon become a widow. However, Consciousness, the "Father within" continues to guide you in your dance through Infinity. Your individual spirit has an interdimensional reality that is heightened in your awareness of your spiritual consciousness. Consciousness continues, and so continues the journey of your Spirit in its return Home. "Be still and know that I AM God". Once your eyes turn inward, you will always long to return. There is a better way to live through Stillness and The Quantum Life!

Re-order your life by joining me in being a divine soldier so together we can live a Divine life. You are an energy Being. You are Divine Life in human form. There is something vast and luminous within you. Use your divine energy to liberate your soul because your only purpose for being on earth is to grow your soul. Through earnest application of listening to your inner voice, you will experience your divine individuality and eventual self-realization. You will live with your soul's rhythm. Learn to live and breathe in this rhythm moment-to-moment. What you get through this process give to others as I am giving to you through this book.

I am sharing my knowledge because all I have left to do in this life cycle is to teach all that I know to help you go back to your Light body. You do what you will with it. I invite you to join me in the Infinite Vast with a focus that our world will become more illumining and more fulfilling by each one attaining spiritual solvency and self-mastery. My own search is not concluded. Join with me in learning the language of Infinity so that together we can return to that perfect Light body both for life and for death. Approach Source. Reshuffle the Stardust. May The Quantum Life provide you with a transcendent life changing power. Welcome to the Movement.

Infinite Pranam

I AM
THE LIGHT
OF
THE WORLD

RESOURCES AND CREDITS PAGE

RESOURCES

Visit www.TheQuantumLife.net to access the many offerings of Dr. M. Teri Daunter, including remote, one-to-one Reiki training, meditation recordings, a selection of her life improving books and to browse her inspirational original art.

CREDITS

Thank you to my talented daughter, Kelly D. Daunter, Ph.D. for editing my book.

Front cover design by Paul Thompson in Petoskey, Michigan.

Flying swan photo (front cover) purchased from Joshua Clark of www.momentsinature.com.

Sitting swans photos (front cover) resourced from public domain.

Award-winning front cover photo captured by Dr. M. Teri Daunter, "Azure Window in Gozo, Malta in the Mediterranean."

Chakra photo, page 182, courtesy of Paul and Daphne Thompson.

"Everything Visible is Empty", page 74, and Reiki symbol, page 205, are original art of Dr. M. Teri Daunter.

Made in the USA
Monee, IL
12 June 2021

71041232R10142